UNLOCKING THE
MYSTERY OF
BABYLON

FROM GENESIS TO END-TIME REVELATION

AMBASSADOR JUSTIN DOUZIECH

UNLOCKING THE MYSTERY OF BABYLON
Copyright © 2023 WAFC Publishing

Paperback ISBN: 979-8-9884669-2-5

Note to reader: There are many words that are **bold** to emphasize what is being pointed out. There are some words that are bold or are in parentheses within Scriptures that are not in the original text. Again, I repeat, please pay special attention and extra care to the **bold** words as they are bold so you may **consider them important to what is being said**. Ultimately, they will cause you to see that **more is to be had** than what we presently have spiritually.

Printed in the United States.

Grateful

I wish to thank and honor my wife, Evelyn, for her help and her input in this book. She has worked with me for many years, and we together have received revelations of Scriptures that have been included in various parts of this book. So, I bless her and thank her.

I also would like to thank those who have helped us along the way in our spiritual walk. We thank the Lord and the Holy Spirit for all revelations.

May the Lord give you more understanding and revelation in the knowledge of Him as you read this book. May we all progress in spiritual maturity.

Contents

Our Scriptures

Isaiah 62:10, "Go through, go through the gates; prepare ye the way of the people; cast up, cast up the highway; gather out the stones; lift up a standard for the people."

Zephaniah 2:1–3, "Gather yourselves together, yea, gather together, O nation not desired; [Those not of Israel] Before the decree bring forth, *before* the day pass as the chaff, before the fierce anger of the LORD come upon you, before the day of the LORD's anger come upon you. Seek ye the LORD, **all ye meek of the earth**, which have wrought his judgment; seek righteousness, seek meekness: it may be **ye shall be hid** in the day of the LORD's anger" (emphasis added).

When I use the word, *we*, I am referring to those who long for more of God. To clarify the use of the word *man*, it refers to mankind and not a male or a female person.

Book 2 in the End Time Series exposes how the world is influenced and controlled by Babylon. Why is Babylon mentioned in the Book of Genesis to the Book of Revelation? Who is Babylon? How has she affected mankind throughout history? Is Babylon a real present-day threat? How does it affect the souls of men? What will God do with Babylon? Who is Babylon? are you part of Babylon?

The book exposes how the world is influenced and controlled by Babylon. Why is Babylon mentioned in Revelation?

Introduction to Babylon

I am writing this book out of love and interest in my fellow Christians for their spiritual growth so they may be able to overcome any and all opposition that we may face in the days ahead.

Who is Babylon physically and whom does she represent spiritually? She appears to be spiritual but hinders her followers' spiritual growth. Since she is spiritual, mankind believes that she has the true way to attain salvation. Is mankind deceived by her?

If the five-fold ministry of the apostle, prophet, teacher, evangelist, and pastor were functioning properly, the people would discern the Babylonian deception and escape her. Then they would not be hindered and could grow spiritually. How is she hindering her followers? Is God the same yesterday, today, and forever, or did He change?

Ultimately this will lead us back to where Adam and Eve were spiritually before they were deceived and fell into sin. What they were before their sin will again be restored to mankind. This is all contained in the restitution of all things which Scripture tells us.

There is a woman in Revelation chapter twelve and she has a son and this son is caught up to heaven yet it is born on the earth. Is this the Antichrist, the followers of Jesus, or an Overcomer? Who are the Overcomers and what is their ministry?

Scripture tells us that Zion has daughters. Who are they? Do they affect us?

Revelation chapter seventeen speaks of another woman, a second woman, who influences the world. Is mankind entrapped by her? When she falls will man's kingdoms also fall with her?

Initially, I was told that Babylon was referring to the Roman Catholic Church. I wanted to see if the Roman Church was truly the **totality of Babylon** as I had been told. Was Babylon more than the Roman Church?

9

Thus, began my quest to understand Babylon. Is it widespread in other religious circles? And what about businesses since the Scriptures bring Babylon into other aspects of the world other than religion?

The Roman Catholic Church started around three hundred years after Jesus Christ's death when the Roman political system under Constantine (February 27, 280 CE–May 22, 337 CE) with his leaders, set up a pope during the First Council of Nacaea in 325 CE. The pope had power and authority with the king. Constantine, the king, was then in control of the people both politically and spiritually. This gave Constantine power over the people concerning matters of heaven and earth since he ordained the pope.

Here is a background history of the Roman Church. The First Council of Nacaea in 325 CE made many changes that affected Christianity. For instance, Constantine, with the Pope changed the Sabbath days from Saturday to Sunday. They then eliminated the Holy Feast days that God had established and substituted them with pagan feasts and gave them new names that sounded Christian. The Roman Church introduced many new rituals, feasts, and new Roman commandments along with changing the Ten Commandments of God. The Roman Church did not want any opposition as they wanted to have **power over the public**. They ruled with the threat of sending someone to hell instead of going to heaven. Public adherence was forced on the people by the military.

Later, there were individuals who rose up to question the Pope's position, the Roman Catholic rituals, and scriptural understandings. In the following centuries, many moves of God followed.

The pope always wanted to control all people without question up until recently.

Demonic spirits influenced this controlling evilness. What was this evil influence? And where did it originate?

Because King James VIII wanted to divorce his wife in 1533, he broke away from the Roman man-made Catholic Church. King James's **political and military** systems gave him power and authority to form the church of England, which he became the head of it. King James had the Bible translated into English and gave the Bible to the people in their language.

In all these situations, God was moving to mature His people as they received the written Word of God to read for themselves. It was a sin to read the Bible in the Roman Catholic Church for many years until recently. Since most people could not read or write, the **church could easily control them**. The Roman church with its **man-made commandments** had control over the rich and the poor, using "being able to go to heaven" as a weapon to control everyone.

It is a serious misunderstanding of history to suppose that the Reformation sprang up entirely from religious motives. But even though social, economic, and political causes played an important part in the origin and progress of the Reformation, one can still believe that its ultimate cause was God's providence.

The reason is that God's creation now had access to Scriptures. They were now potentially growing spiritually. They were going from glory to glory. They went from no scripture to having scripture. Later, through many moves of God, many people were born again. Then there were the moves of the infilling of the Holy Ghost, then healings and miracles, and today the people desire to have the presence and the glory of God.

Roman Catholics frequently refer to the Reformation as the "Protestant revolt." They look upon it as a revolt against the authority of the pope and the church, and thus a revolt against God. Certainly, it was a revolt against Rome, but it was a **turning to God** from the evils and corruption of the Roman system.

The Roman Church persecuted many true Christians in her past wars. Some people say that the Roman Catholic Church is Babylon because, in her past, many people were killed and persecuted under her direction forcing the public to adhere to her teachings.

In 2018, there are still misconceptions about the Roman Catholic Church. Today, some call her Babylon because the city is built on seven hills. This is false because Revelation 17:19 says "mountains" (Strong Concordance #3735), not hills.

Babylon is also supposed to be in all the countries of the world according to Revelation 14:8, but the Roman Church is not in all the countries of the earth. Nor did she exist in the Old Testament.

Revelation 14:8, "And there followed another angel, saying, **Babylon** is fallen, is fallen, that great city, because she made **all nations** drink of the wine of the wrath of her fornication" (emphasis added).

Nor did Babylon kill all the people that Revelation speaks of. We need to see what the Bible has to say about Babylon, who she is, and who killed many people in the world.

The Roman Church **did not exist** in the Old Testament but Babylon did. Zechariah 2:7 tells us, "Deliver thyself, O Zion, that dwellest with the daughters of Babylon."

Zechariah tells us to deliver ourselves from the daughters of Babylon, but the Roman church did not exist at that time. The spirit of Babylon did exist. Therefore, Babylon is something else.

Nor did the Roman Church kill all the prophets that Jesus was referring to in Luke 11:47 since it did not exist at that time.

Luke 11:47, "Woe unto you! for ye build the sepulchres of the prophets, and your fathers killed them."

Who did the killing? It was the religious Jewish leaders. It was that Babylonian Spirit that was operating in these evil leaders.

We will also examine the time of Jesus when the religious Jews, using their followers and their powers to execute their will, had Jesus condemned. Then they use the Roman Gentile political-military system to crucify Jesus. The Jewish leaders condemned Jesus and the Gentile Roman soldiers crucified Him. They were all guilty of His death. Many early Jewish Christian church leaders were beaten or martyred because they believed in Jesus. The religious persecuted the true believers, even the Apostle Paul persecuted believers before his conversion.

As we can see, Babylon is much more than the Roman Catholic Church. The Roman Church has the Babylonian spirit in her, but she is in no way the totality of Babylon.

Is Babylon only in religious circles? Is she also in business? And if so, how? How is this possible since most businesses are not involved with religion? or are they? We shall see if Babylon is involved in businesses. This search led me to have a greater understanding of the book of Revelation, the last book in the Bible. Who are all these symbols?

Who or what is the woman of Revelation chapters 2 and 12 depicting? During the period of time spoken of in the book of Revelation, will there be any true believers on the earth at this time? Will God have spiritually mature people? What will God's followers be doing? These are some of the topics this book series will reveal and help you in your study for spiritual growth.

As we delve into these topics, let us remember to **separate the systems of religion and the people within the systems**. I will bring some understanding of these Bible passages using Scriptures as I expound on these Scriptures as much as possible. We will be using the King James Bible as our main reference book for quoted Scriptures.

We have to understand **types and shadows** to understand the truths behind some of these Scriptures which will be examined.

Luke 8:10, "And he said, Unto you it is given to know the mysteries of the kingdom of God: but to others in parables; that seeing they might not see, and hearing they might not understand." (See also Matthew 13:11)

First Corinthians 10:11, "Now all these things happened unto them [it was reality for them] for ensamples [symbols, types for us]: and they are written for our admonition, upon **whom the ends of the world** are come" (emphasis added).

Since it appears as though we are living in the end times, it is extremely important that we understand the times and that we grow up spiritually. We need to understand the symbols of the Bible which pertain to the end times. **Spiritual maturity is what will keep God's people above the situations that are happening on Earth.** Please be open to receiving a new understanding of these symbols which will be a source of great encouragement.

Today, in our church system of denominations, we need to understand that God is using them to varying degrees. Some have no presence of God, and no light, while others have some presence and some light. God is using denominations today, but because of their indifference toward the five-fold ministry of apostles, prophets, evangelists, teachers, and pastors, they are limited as to how mature the people within them can become. Some groups have some manifestations of God while others have no godly supernatural manifestations of any kind. This has left various groups open to spiritual manifestations that are not of God.

Some churches are in grade one, spiritually speaking, and some are in grade two, while others are in grade four in spiritual maturity. You may have a revival at any one of these levels, but we individually or as a church have not reached grade twelve in maturity, but we must. Some must mature to fulfill Scripture and the prayers of Jesus. I pray that we are that generation.

This book will examine several questions that need to be answered to understand how Babylon corrupted the original intentions of God to this day.

Was mankind going to be faithful to God or was man going to decide for himself who to worship and how to worship?

Was he going to go God's way or was he going to be rebellious and confused as he developed his own ways of who and how to worship God? And what god was he going to worship?

Is this rebellion still on Earth? And if it is, how is it influencing us today?

What was going to happen to mankind in his rebellion?

When did this rebellion start?

Does the Bible speak of this rebellion? And what will be the outcome?

What will happen to those who have not followed those who have rebelled?

Does the book of Revelation reveal anything concerning this rebellion to us?

Will mankind ever be spiritually mature to fulfill the Scriptures?

Can we discern during this onslaught of lies and new false points of view?

Can we discern the times we live in?

Will God's people be on the earth during the end days?

These questions, along with others, will be answered as you read. I pray that you will be greatly blessed and enlightened as you read. May the truths of God that are in this book be revealed and become pitchers of silver and apples of gold to you.

If there are revelations that are hard to understand, please keep on reading, for there are many other truths in this book that will bring light to the Scriptures for you. The Scriptures that are unfamiliar to you, please put them on a mental shelf for revelation at a future time.

This series of three books will establish an understanding of certain facts in order to start to understand the book of Revelations.

Please pay special attention and extra care to the **bold** words as they are bold so you may consider them **important to what is being said**. Ultimately, they will cause you to see that **more is to be had** spiritually than what we presently have.

CHAPTER 1

Babylon

Physical Babylon

Why is Babylon mentioned from Genesis to the book of Revelation? Why does scripture use the word *Babylon*? What does Babylon mean?

The word *Babel* first appears in Genesis 10:8–10.

Genesis 10:8–10, "And Cush begat Nimrod: he **began to be** [morphed] a mighty one in the earth,

"He was a mighty hunter before the LORD: wherefore it is said, Even as Nimrod the mighty hunter before the LORD.

"And the beginning of **his kingdom was Babel**, and Erech, and Accad, and Calneh, in the land of Shinar" (emphasis added).

In Genesis 11:4–5, the pompous leaders say, "**let us build us a city and a tower whose top may reach into the heaven;** and let us **make us a name**, lest we be scattered abroad upon the face of the whole earth. And the LORD came down to see the city and the tower, which the children of men built" (emphasis added).

Babel (in the Strong Concordance #H895,) appears 246 times in the Old Testament. However, it only appears eight times in the New Testament, and six of those are in the book of Revelation.

Webster's Dictionary says that Babylon was a city devoted to **materialism** and the pursuit of **sensual pleasure**. It was a beautiful city with hanging gardens and was a center for many **religious gods**.

One of the highlights of the city of Babylon was for its **religious gods**, which it typifies. It had a main gate named after Ishtar, a goddess. In the city was a temple to Marduk, the creator god and the king of the universe. In ancient writing, the word *Babylon* referred to astrologers such as the Chaldeans who used divine powers. Chaldeans were in all or in part of Babylon depending on the time considered. They were into witchcraft.

God was disturbed by what the men of Babylon were attempting to build. During the construction of the Tower of Babel, God supernaturally mixed the people's language into many languages in order to stop the construction. **Thus, Babylon implies mixed, confused a**s the people's language was mixed and brought confusion and much chaos. Babel means confused. Babylon was a city whose people had a relationship with false gods or witchcraft. This brought confusion to them as to the truth of how to worship the true God.

Ezekiel 21:21–22 "For the **king of Babylon** stood at the parting of the way, at the head of the two ways, to **use divination**: he made his arrows bright, he consulted with images, he looked in the liver. At his right hand was the divination for Jerusalem" (emphasis added).

Here the **King of Babylon** is consulting **divination**, seeking knowledge, but not from God. We are not to use any form of divination or witchcraft. God established how to consult the supernatural. We are to seek power, wisdom, and direction from God alone. We can read how Daniel sought God the right way in the Book of Daniel.

Daniel 2:19, "Then was the secret revealed unto Daniel in a night vision. Then Daniel **blessed the God of heaven**" (emphasis added).

Babylon also had a tower or a man-made mountain for which the city is known. The Tower of Babel was man trying to exalt himself to the heavens to the place of God. The Babylonian leaders of the city were trying to build a mountain in order to lift themselves up into **the place** of God as a god. They wanted to be seated in the place of God, replacing God. They wanted to be a god. This is the same as what the serpent told Eve in Genesis 3:5.

Genesis 3:5, "For God doth know that in the day ye eat thereof, then your eyes shall be opened, and ye shall be as gods, knowing good and evil."

We can easily see that the mountain the wicked people were building was called a ziggurat which Satan attempted to copy and to replace

God. God has a mountain which he dwells in as we see in Revelation chapter twenty-one. Satan wanted to lift himself to the place of God and he was using man to accomplish his goal.

In some circles today, it is believed that a portal, an opening into **another dimension,** existed at the location of the Babylonian Tower. That is why that specific location was chosen to build this man-made edifice. Through this portal, the leaders hoped to attain a higher level of the supernatural for themselves. Are we attempting to do the same today with man's Large Hadron Collider which is in Switzerland?

Today, in some parts of the world such as in Arizona, some natives claim to have access to a portal from which beings from another dimension manifest on occasion. They are very secretive as to where and when these manifestations happen. They are very real to them.

God mixed the language of the people in Babylon while they were building their ziggurat, and great confusion came upon the people. The confusion that followed forced them to abandon the construction of the monument. Thus, the city became known as Babylon, which exemplifies **confusion** along with its many false gods.

Why did God intervene in Babylon? It was not because they were doing the will of God. They were confused when they were lifted up in their own minds as to who God is, who is in control, and how man is to fellowship with God.

Man has always wanted to exalt himself to the place of God. He exalts himself when he, using his mind, decides for himself how to do things. He wants to decide for himself how to reach God and how to live.

Babylon was a city. A city is a man-made center where man is in control. It is a place that **man has created**, developed, and built. It is his **man-made glory**. A city is the glory of man rather than the glory of God. This is the **man-made glory** that Jesus was tempted with by Satan after He was baptized in the river Jordan by John the Baptist. (Matthew 4:8)

Matthew 4:8, "Again, the devil taketh him up into an exceeding high mountain, and sheweth him all the kingdoms of the world, and the glory of them."

Now we come to understand that **Babylon represents man lifting himself up to the place of God,** using his own mind and or using other supernatural powers other than God's power. Man uses idols, false gods, and other forms of worship other than God's way to attain **supernatu-**

ral manifestations and power. Man uses his thinking to make decisions without consulting God. Man wants to sit on the throne of his life without God.

In Daniel 4:22, we read that King Nebuchadnezzar, king of Babylon, made an idol, which was probably of himself since he was full of pride and wanted to be exalted. The idol was lifted up as a god which was to be worshipped by all.

In Babylon we see mankind building a tower, wanting to lift himself up to heaven using **"the way" that "he" wants rather than God's way.** He decides to build a tower to reach the heavens. They wanted to be exalted as God with all of his power and glory. This heavenly entrance would enable the leaders to get greater knowledge and power. They would have gotten power over other men, But God considered them as children.

Babylon is mentioned many times in the Bible. Some of the books use the word Babylon to mean or to emphasize **different aspects** of Babylon.

God's Way of Worship

God had established the way to come before Him from the beginning. After Adam and Eve sinned, many things were altered. The earth changed and many spiritual elements were altered. Adam and Eve were afraid of the voice of God since they could no longer come before Him as before. Sin had to be dealt with. God killed the first animal to cover Adam and Eve both physically and spiritually. He used the skins to cover their physical nakedness and the animals shed blood to cover their sin spiritually. This was clearly showing mankind what man had to do to **cover his sins in order to come before God.**

They did the rituals but God was interested in their heart to see if they loved Him and that they were doing the commandments out of love and not out of rituals. Grace was the issue.

Genesis 3:21, "Unto Adam also and to his wife did the LORD **God make coats of skins, and clothed them**" (emphasis added).

God had previously finished creation therefore He had to take the skins from an animal that He had previously created. I speculate that the animal was a lamb, the symbol of Jesus, as an offering.

Hebrews 9:22, "For without the shedding of blood there is no remission of sin."

Sin came forth because Adam and Eve **decided** to listen to the serpent, setting themselves on the **throne of their lives** as a king and queen. When they made that decision, they thereby rejected God as their leader. They forsook God's command which was to have and take dominion over all the earth, which included the serpent. They **forsook that authority** and let the serpent take over as he talked to Eve. Adam was fully aware of what was going on since **he was not deceived** and was right there with Eve. He let the serpent speak or should I say, lie and control the situation. Since Adam forsook his God-given authority, he could never go before God as before.

Genesis 3:17, "And unto Adam he said, Because thou hast **hearkened unto the voice of thy wife**, and hast eaten of the tree, of which **I commanded thee**, saying, Thou shalt **not** eat of it: cursed *is* the ground for thy sake; in sorrow shalt thou eat *of* it all the days of thy life" (emphasis added).

First Timothy 2:14, "And **Adam was not deceived**, but the woman, having been deceived, into transgression came" (emphasis added).

Romans 6:16, "Know ye not, that to **whom ye yield** yourselves **servants to obey**, his **servants ye are** to whom ye obey; whether of sin unto death, or of obedience unto righteousness?" (emphasis added).

We can clearly see that building a tower to heaven was not the way to come before God nor was it going to be successful.

Who is Babylon Prophetically?

Babylon implies using **evil powers** and is paralleled with the Chaldeans who were soothsayers who used witchcraft. It is one who deals with supernatural powers that are not of God. It is one who makes decisions without consulting God. This is removing God from His rightful position.

Babylon means **confusion**, not doing, or not knowing the right way, not knowing the truth. It is **anything that takes away from the true way and true worship of God.** It is failing to recognize that God is God and that He is above all and should be **involved in all things and in all deci-**

sion-making. He is Lord, Boss, and King.

Babylon is, in part, a symbol of the things of this world as was Babylon that are in the **form of religion** and take the place of a **true relationship** with the only true God. Babylon or religions are all over the world as Revelation 18:23 tells us, "by thy sorceries were **all nations** deceived" (emphasis added).

Babylon is also the spirit of wickedness and is against God's people since it wants to be **exalted to the place of God**. She hates and kills God's people.

Who killed "all" that were slain upon the earth as Revelation 18:24 reads, "And in her [Babylon] was found the blood of prophets, and of saints, and of **all that were slain** upon the earth" (emphasis added).

Who is Babylon referring to in the book of Revelation? Who killed "all" the people of God during the past centuries is one of the main questions to answer. Since the word *all* is used, we need to go back to Adam and Eve. It cannot apply just to the city of Babylon or the Roman Catholic Church since it did not exist at the beginning.

Adam **lifted himself up** in his mind and decided he wanted to know between right and wrong. He wanted knowledge he had not been given. He wanted to know good and evil. Knowing about evil could not be good. What was involved in knowing evil? Did it involve witchcraft since that is what God considers evil? Adam decided to let the serpent talk rather than take his God-given authority and tell the serpent to be quiet and leave. He forsook God's command to take his authority thus **sinning as he sat on the throne of his life**.

After Adam's first sin, we read of Cain and Abel.

Genesis 4:3–5, "And in process of time it came to pass, that Cain brought of the fruit of the ground an offering unto the LORD

"And Abel, he also brought of the firstlings of his flock and of the fat thereof. And the LORD **had respect unto Abel and to his offering**:

"But unto **Cain and to his offering he had not respect**. And Cain was very wroth, and his countenance fell" (emphasis added).

Abel offered the right sacrifice, an animal sacrifice, but Cain offered his fruit of the earth. He did **what "he" wanted to offer, his way of worship**. He sat on the throne of his life instead of God. He made the decision on his own as to what he thought God should accept. His decision on how to worship is that **Babylonian**, that religious spirit that says **"I"**

will decide what God will accept. He offered the **best of his fruit** of the ground and **with all of his heart**, but it was not how God would receive a sacrifice from man. Cain, the religious, became jealous and killed righteous Abel who did the will of God. To be religious is the foundation of most religions of the earth.

First John 3:12, "Not as Cain, *who* was of that wicked one, and slew his brother. And wherefore slew he him? Because his own works were evil, and his brother's righteous."

The **religious people** of Israel in the Old Testament and not the true people of God, killed the prophets according to Jesus. Luke 11:47, "Woe unto you! For ye [Jewish religious leaders] build the sepulchers of the prophets and **your fathers killed them**" (emphasis added). (See also Matthew 23:31, 37)

During the time of Jesus, John the Baptist was killed by the man-made political-military system, the Roman Empire. He was righteous and a prophet of God. He was in jail because he stood for the laws of God.

Today in America, we do not usually kill. But after we, on our own, have decided what should be done, we pray, or should I say we dictate orders to God for God to respond to. Or we do our own works and tell God to bless our work. Most of the time, when decisions are made, **God is not consulted at all**. Man is on the **throne of his life** with no consideration of God's will for the situation at hand. This applies to most businesses also.

Who Are the Ones Noted for the Killing of Many of God's People?

Here are some historical facts to examine. Hitler, a Satanist who was involved with witchcraft who killed many people. Amongst them were many Jews, Christians, and others. Hitler was demon-possessed and had his own false prophet.

China has killed millions of Christians because they were Christians. They also killed many who had any form of religion and who opposed their man-made assumed supreme leadership. To some extent, it still happens today.

And now we are killing millions of babies through abortions all over the world as man decides whether to keep the infant or not, regardless of God's desire. In the Old Testament days, babies were killed or burned as they were given to their false gods. Who is indirectly in charge of these atrocities? **It is mankind under evil influence**.

Islam is a religion that was developed by a man. Muslims are killing tens of thousands of Christians and others in Africa today and in other parts of the world because of their faith. They even kill one another. Who directs this wickedness? It is men who make the decision to kill or to let live as if they are God? They are as a god in their own minds. They mistreat their woman as slaves making them do certain rituals such as the face covering for no good reason.

Man exalts himself, lifting himself to the place of God, then goes and decides on his own to kill others who do not desire to follow their beliefs or way of life. Today, there are over 4,500 religions founded in the world since the start of recorded history. Each one was started by men, except one, God's given religion. Each religion believes they are the ultimate right way. This is mankind sitting on the **throne of his life**, deciding what God needs to accept. **That is that Babylonian spirit in these religious**. This is the religious Babylonian spirit because it is man making decisions instead of seeking the true living God to see what He has to say or has commanded. This brings great confusion to God's creation. This is Babylon.

Hindrances of Religion

Today, man-made religions are all over the world. They hinder the true Word of God from going forth to all the earth. They stop the true seekers, the true followers from finding the deeper truths of God and from spiritually maturing. Because of these religious hindrances, the whole world suffers.

Zechariah 5:3, 7, 8, 11. Zechariah supports what we are saying:

Verse 3, "this is the curse that goeth forth over the face of the whole earth."

Zechariah 5:7, 8, "this is a woman…[Babylon] this is wickedness [Exalted man, controlling others]."

Zechariah 5:11, "to build it a house in the land of Shinar."

Shinar is Babylon. As Babylon built a place for their gods, we today build buildings in worldly ways and call them houses of God. They are not. The people of God are the house of God.

Babylon Is not Alone

She has daughters as we shall see.

In Jeremiah 51:33, "For thus saith the LORD of hosts, the God of Israel; The daughter of Babylon *is* like a threshingfloor, *it is* time to thresh her: yet a little while, and the time of her harvest shall come."

Zechariah 2:7 also tell us of Babylon having daughters, "Deliver thyself, O Zion, that dwellest with the daughters of Babylon."

Babylon has many daughters. There are many that do Babylon's bidding, many false religions, false religious groups, full of lies and wickedness, wanting to control God's creation wanting to steal souls. They are all over the earth. These religious groups are full of man-made traditions. Daughters represent the many various **arms of religion** that are throughout the world who do the work of Babylon, the mother.

Zechariah is saying to the people of God to **separate themselves** from the daughters of Babylon."

Isaiah 47:1, "Come down, and sit in the dust, O **virgin daughter of Babylon**, sit on the ground: *there is* **no throne**, O **daughter** of the **Chaldeans**: for thou shalt no more be called tender and delicate" (emphasis added).

These daughters get their power and authority from the beast. The beast, at the time of Jesus, was the wicked spiritual influential power of the man-made political-military systems that ruled the earth. The wicked men, these religious leaders got their power and authority from man's political and military system, the Roman leaders. This was the God of force. They deny the lordship of Jesus Christ. These religious leaders used this power to condemn Jesus Christ. Then the religious leaders went to the Gentile Romans to use their power to execute the crucifixion of Jesus. The Roman leader found no fault in Jesus.

Still, the religious Jews still demanded His execution, so the Romans condemned Him and crucified Him. This shows us the power that this **religious spirit** has over men. This is the religious condemning the righteous. The Roman decision-making or man making decisions on his own without discernment, is religion, Babylon. As they lifted themselves up to the place of God on the **throne of their life**, they decided to condemn Jesus to death. This is the spirit of wickedness because it condemns to death a person for no righteous cause. Babylon has had many killed all over the earth in the past centuries. **This demonic Babylonian spirit is after the souls of men, regardless of how they are acquired.**

Revelation 18:2, "And he cried mightily with a strong voice, saying, Babylon the great is fallen, is fallen, and is become the habitation of devils, and the hold of every foul spirit, and a cage of every unclean and hateful bird."

Does this mean that all the religions of the world and man-made businesses will come to their end as Babylon falls?

Babylon will eventually be removed from her throne ruling position. She will be cast down and destroyed according to Revelation 18:2, 21. She is called the daughter of the Chaldeans because the Chaldeans were into witchcraft as is Babylon.

According to 1 Timothy 6:10, the root of evil is money which man has invented.

John 12:43 says, "They love the praise of men more than the praises of God."

Why? Because it **exalts man** as to how great he is instead of God being great."

CHAPTER 2

Deception in Babylon

Escape from Babylon

Today, in the United States, the political governmental powers give the churches their authority to marry, have buildings, be a non-profit organization, and more, or the government can fine you or shut you down. Some groups have been shut down because the government did not agree with them, though the groups were justified. In many countries, the government holds power over the people as to what to preach. In some countries, churches and church buildings are taxed, while in other countries, they are tax-exempt according to their man-made laws.

Babylon is mankind making decisions that are motivated by evil spirits. This is mankind who decides for himself what to do as if he is God. This is man making himself God while controlling religious followers as is done all over the world. These religious leaders are exalted in their own minds, confused, and deceived. This applies to every religion, including atheism, and every cult in the world. This is mankind exalting "himself" to the place of God and is just being religious.

Mankind is inventing all kinds of ways to worship his god, but in so doing, he is full of darkness, full of spirits, full of wickedness, and confused about the true way to worship God as was Cain. This is Babylon, confusion as a religious spirit.

An example I have heard of is of an Arabian man who had a hand cut off from his maid because she had stolen something from him. This is a Muslim penalty for stealing. It did not matter that he had not paid her for years, was raping her, and that she was trying to get away, but he would not let her go. These man-made laws are wickedness and are in every man-made religion in varying degrees.

This is also true for those who have known the right way of worshipping God and then have backslidden. These backslidden people often fall into rituals rather than developing a deeper personal relationship with God. The true people of God have an ever-increasing relationship with Him. They go from grade one to grade twelve, spiritually speaking.

This spirit of Babylon is witchcraft and it is manipulating, controlling, deceiving, and stealing from people using various powers, including personal charisma. This spirit is used by many religious leaders. These leaders, using this spirit, have power over individuals as well as over groups. They use this spirit for their own benefit. These religious leaders exalt themselves to the place of God. They exalt themselves above other people, lording it over others. This happens in all religions, in the pretense **of protecting their followers** rather than having the people spiritually mature and trusting God for themselves.

Your Covering

Some say that followers need a covering. They ask, "Who is your **covering**?" Others say, "Go see that leader and he will pray for your healing." Or "Go see that medicine man and he will pray for you." They thereby build their names, and their ministries, and exalt these leaders and their kingdoms.

Yes, we can go to your godly spiritual leaders, but we need to grow up and become mature. To stay immature is not of God and is wickedness. Let the Lord be Lord. He is Lord of all. He is our healer and the only God we are to follow.

We see this also in the Old Testament, how in the book of Hosea, Ephraim exalted himself.

In Hosea 13:1, we read the following: "When Ephraim spoke trembling, he exalted himself in Israel, but when he offended in **Baal he died**" (emphasis added).

Baal was a false god. What made Ephraim exalt himself? When

Ephraim exalted himself, he took the place of God. He still recognized God, but not in proper order. But when he started to worship Baal, an idol, a false god, he was spiritually dead and died. Here, he is as a man, deciding how and whom to worship, rather than obeying what God had instituted. This is the spirit of wickedness. This is the spirit of Babylon.

Babylon is not to be in the people of the true church of Jesus Christ who have a true personal relationship with Father God. Most of the Christian religious groups of today started right, but years later, they are in deception and are caught up in man's thinking, man's rituals, and man-made commandments. This can also be seen in the Old Testament as the people of Israel started right but then moved away from the ways of God. As they moved away from God, the religious leaders and kings became more and more corrupt. This is rebellious man exalted in the place of God, setting up man-made laws, and man's ways, ruling God's creation instead of God. Then these rebellious religious leaders put their people under **their laws and their traditions** as they invent more and more rules. This is putting **people in prison houses**. They are put in a prison house of that religious group or those denominational **teachings**, putting them into bondage to their ways. Their followers are hindered from growing spiritually. This is man ruling over other men, instead of God being over man.

Revelation 18:4, "And I heard another voice from heaven, saying, Come out of her, my people, that ye be not partakers of her sins, and that ye receive not of her plagues."

These people are in **prison houses** because they are caught in these groups and then bound by the laws of these religious leaders. The laws of their religion or their denomination bind them from knowing the true living God. They cannot escape in order to find the true God out of fear of breaking these man-made laws and then being excommunicated or killed, and not being able to go to heaven. These deprived followers are hindered from finding God, knowing more of Him, and moving in the gifts of the Spirit. Their teachings put man between God's people and God.

In some cases, these leaders are honored and esteemed as being the only ones who can go to God. These leaders exalt themselves as being God's only representative. This is man ruling God's creation rather than letting God be their Lord. Is that what God desires? Are we to stay in the strongholds of these religious organizations? This is Babylon who is after these people's souls.

In Revelations 18:4, "the word says: Come **out of her** [Babylon] my people, that ye be not partakers of **her sins**, and that ye receive not of her plagues" (emphasis added).

As you can see, **God has people in Babylon to be calling them out**. At times, God may send you into Babylon to work as He did with Joseph. Joseph was the son of Jacob who was sold as a slave to the Egyptians. Later, he was made a leader in Egypt. He was used by God to save Egypt and God's people, Israel, from destruction during a famine.

Remember that Babylon is the spirit in the religious systems and not necessarily the people within the systems. Some people in the systems are just baby Christians, yet they will grow spiritually to some degree, but then God will call them out to deliver them out of man's grasp unless they do not hunger for more of God. Those who do not hunger will not be delivered and receive more revelation. The people trapped within these groups are people of God and not Satan's followers. They should not be in Babylon. This is why God is calling them out. Let us pray for more of God.

Mankind always seems to want to control others. That is why the spirit of **Babylon is in all religious organizations** and businesses to varying degrees and in many individuals to varying degrees. It is present everywhere unless God sends revelation and delivers that individual. Individually, you and I must want to be delivered **more than once** as we continue to hunger for the heart of God as we grow up spiritually. Then we can fully follow Him. We must make Him the **Lord of all**. We may begin in a certain group, but we are **not to remain** in that group once we start to spiritually mature. We must free ourselves from all these controlling systems if we are to grow up and become **spiritually mature**. We must continue until we enter the **fullness of the very presence of God**, His presence is called Zion.

The book of Zechariah stresses this point. Zechariah 2:7, "Deliver thyself, O Zion, [God's dwelling place which is also within us] that dwellest with the daughters of Babylon. [man-made religions]".

See also daughter of Zion in Zech. 2:10–11).

To "deliver" yourself is to make yourself free.

Jeremiah also confirms this same message in Chapter 51:6, 45, "Flee out of the midst of Babylon, and deliver every man his soul [his own self]" (emphasis added).

To be free, we need to grow spiritually. How much? To the **fullness** of Jesus Christ.

Ephesians 4:13, "Till we all come in the unity of the faith, and of the knowledge of the Son of God, unto a **perfect** man, **unto the measure of the stature of the fulness** of Christ" (emphasis added).

Jeremiah Speaks of Utter Destruction of Babylon

Jeremiah 51:1–12, "Thus saith the LORD; Behold, I will raise up **against** Babylon, and against them that dwell in the midst of them that rise up against me, a destroying wind;

"And will send unto Babylon fanners, that shall fan her, and shall empty her land: for in the day of trouble they shall be against her round about.

"Against *him that* bendeth let the archer bend his bow, and against *him that* lifteth himself up in his brigandine: and spare ye not her young men; destroy ye utterly all her host.

"Thus the slain shall fall in the land of the Chaldeans, and *they that are* thrust through in her streets.

"For Israel *hath* not *been* forsaken, nor Judah of his God, of the LORD of hosts; though their land was filled with sin against the Holy One of Israel.

"**Flee out** of the midst of Babylon, and deliver every man his soul: be not cut off in her iniquity; for this *is* the **time of the LORD's vengeance**; he will render unto her a recompence.

"Babylon *hath been* a golden cup in the LORD's hand, that **made all the earth drunken**: the nations have drunken of her wine; therefore the nations are mad.

"**Babylon is suddenly fallen and destroyed**: howl for her; take balm for her pain, if so be she may be healed.

"We would have healed Babylon, but she is not healed: forsake her, and let us go every one into his own country: for her judgment reacheth unto heaven, and is lifted up *even* to the skies.

"The LORD hath brought forth our righteousness: come, and let us declare in Zion the work of the LORD our God.

"**Make bright the arrows**; [we are God's arrows] gather the shields: the LORD hath raised up the spirit of the kings of the Medes: for **his de-**

vice *is* **against Babylon, to destroy it**; because it *is* the vengeance of the LORD, the **vengeance of his temple**. [We are God's temple]

"Set up the **standard** upon the walls of Babylon, make the watch strong, set up the watchmen, prepare the ambushes: for the LORD hath both devised and done that which he spake against the inhabitants of Babylon."

God is speaking to His people to deliver their souls from man's religions because God is coming against those religious systems. He is coming against these exalted men who have taken the place of God. He will remove these leaders.

Jeremiah 51:45, "**My people**, go ye out of the midst of her, and deliver ye **every man his soul** from the fierce anger of the Lord" (emphasis added).

See all of chapter 51, especially 7–10.

God is speaking to His people to deliver **their souls from man's religions** because God is coming against those religious systems. He is coming against these exalted men who have taken the place of God. He will remove these men.

God will raise up anointed people to make His people free. God speaks through Isaiah in Isaiah 45:1, "Thus saith the Lord to **his anointed**, to Cyrus whose right hand **I have** holden, to subdue nations before him; and I will loose the loins of kings, to **open before him the two leaved gates; and the gates shall not be shut**" (emphasis added). See also Isaiah 45:1–13.

These gates are the **gates of the religious prison houses**. Prison houses are the religious organizations of the world that control the people Isaiah 34:2 continues, "I will go before thee, and make the crooked places straight: I will break in pieces the **gates of brass** and cut asunder the **bars of iron**" (emphasis).

Cyrus means heir. God will give His anointed heirs the spirit of Revelation and Truth so they may see and discern rightly.

Iron is the symbol of laws. The law is stiff and rigid. The Old Testament was the law that kept the people in bondage, in prison to the system of the man-made laws by which they enforced their religion. The Bible says the law could make **nothing perfect** and thereby kept the people immature and spiritually in prison. They were to attain salvation by faith and not by works. They were to have a heart for God. They were to do the rituals out of love for God and not try to attain salvation by their good works.

Hebrews 7:19, "For the **law made nothing perfect**, but the bringing in of a better hope *did;* by the which **we draw nigh unto God**" (emphasis added).

Brass means judgment and refers to the New Testament of grace. Present-day churches and their man-made laws keep the people within them in prison. They are in prison, because in this age of Grace, we operate "**in part**." We prophesied in part and we see through a glass darkly. Many people use "Grace" to justify their sinful way of life. They are deceived.

First Corinthian 13:9–13 "For we know in part, and we prophesy **in part.**

"But when that which is **perfect is come**, [mature as Jesus] then that which is in part shall be done away.

"When I was a child, I spoke **as a child**, I understood as a child, I thought as a child: but when **I became a man**, [growing up] I put away childish things.

"For **now [New Testament] we see** through a glass, darkly; but **then [future] face to face**: now I know in part; **but then** shall I know even as also I am known.

"**Till** [until] we all come in the unity of the faith, and of the knowledge of the Son of God, unto a perfect man, unto the **measure of the stature** of the **fulness of Christ**" (emphasis added).

If you try to get salvation by **doing the rituals,** you are not going to attain it, because no man could fulfill the law. **You had to come by faith, even in the Old Testament**. It has always been by faith. You had to come believing and trusting in God for your salvation and not in doing the rituals or good works.

Today, we have many religions that have made many laws that keep people in bondage, in prison houses. They say, "You do what we say, or you will be lost." Others say, "You must have our covering," while others say, "You must stay in this religious group or this church." The people are in bondage because they have the desire to find God, be saved, and go to heaven. But these man-made laws are as rigid as iron, **keeping its followers behind bars**, keeping them from going on into the deeper truths of God. By the grace of God and faith in God, we are saved and not by the works of the law. This applies to the Old and the New Testaments. God by faith saves us just because He loves us. He sent His Son to deliver us and pay for our sins. We must accept Him as our Savior and rest in that fact by faith. This is how our spiritual journey begins. We must learn to trust the Lord for and in all situations as He matures us.

The New Testament is represented by the bars of brass. We come in by "Grace." The New Testament is **only in part and is not complete or perfect**. Those under Grace have not, to this day, entered into the **fullness of Jesus Christ**. We must continue our spiritual walk until the fullness of Grace is apprehended and we fully enter. Unfortunately, many Christian churches are part Law and part Grace, and thereby the people are hindered. The people should be free to enter into all that Grace has to offer, which brings total deliverance. This must happen, and it is **not going** to happen when we are in heaven but here on Earth.

Let us find the deep truths. Isaiah 45:3, "And I will give thee, the **treasures** of darkness and hidden riches of secret places, that thou mayest know that I, the Lord, which call thee **by thy name**, am the God of Israel" (emphasis added).

Spiritual revelations of the truths of God are hidden deep from natural view and can only be found by sincere searching in prayer. These truths will be revealed to the heirs as they seek God and receive an anointing. Who are the heirs? God started with natural Israel but now desires all men to follow Him, regardless of race. God knows us intimately and calls us by our personal name.

Isaiah 45:13, "I have raised him [Jesus, Cyrus, anointed ones] up in righteousness and **I will** direct all his ways: he shall **build my city**, [New Jerusalem, bring souls in] and he shall **let go my captives** [those who are still immature and in prison houses], not for price nor reward, [not by good works but by the Spirit of God] saith the Lord of host" (emphasis added).

The heirs, the true believers, are raised or matured. To mature means to grow up spiritually and **be anointed** to the fullness of Christ. The heirs will guide and build God's city by bringing others into God's kingdom through the shed blood of Jesus. By the anointing upon them and by the Spirit of the Holy Ghost, they will be made free.

The mature anointed ones will deliver God's people from their prison houses by revealing the truths. Their eyes will then be open as they receive the Spirit of Truth and the Spirit of Revelation. The anointing of the Spirit is the way of making prisoners free of any and all bondages. The captives are people in man-made religions, sin, and the world but they belong to God and need to be free to grow up. The anointing on the

mature sons will make God's people free to worship and obey God. Free from lust, free from sin, and any other prison house.

God's people will have no interest in building their own personal kingdom or organization. They will not build their own ministry, their own mountain. The people will be free from man's control, free to come to God and find deeper truths. They will be freed from sin and the lust of the flesh, demonic possession, and man-made prison houses of religions. They will desire to free the souls that are trapped in Babylon. Babylon desires the souls of men.

Revelation 18:13, "And cinnamon, and odours, and ointments, and frankincense, and wine, and oil, and fine flour, and wheat, and beasts, and sheep, and horses, and chariots, and slaves, and **souls of men**" (emphasis added).

The writer of Revelation, John, repeats the same calling of coming out of man-made religions, including denominations to find personally the deeper truths.

John, in Revelations 22:17 writes, "And the Spirit and the Bride say, Come. And let **him** that is **athirst come.** And whosoever will, let him take of the **water freely**" (emphasis added).

Setting The Captives Free

Isaiah 44:28, "That saith of Cyrus, *He is* my shepherd, and shall perform all my pleasure: even saying to Jerusalem, Thou shalt be built; and to the temple, Thy foundation shall be laid."

Isaiah 45:1–3, "Thus saith the LORD to his anointed, to Cyrus, whose right hand I have holden, to subdue nations before him; and I will loose the loins of kings, to open before him the two leaved gates; and the gates shall not be shut;

"I will go before thee, and make the crooked places straight: I will break in pieces the gates of brass, and cut in sunder the bars of iron:

"And I will give thee the treasures of darkness, and hidden riches of secret places, that thou mayest know that I, the LORD, which call *thee* by thy name, *am* the God of Israel."

Isaiah 45:13, "I have **raised him up** [Jesus, Overcomers] in righteousness, and **I will direct all his ways: he shall build my city**, and

he shall let go my captives, not for price nor reward, saith the LORD of hosts" (emphasis added).

Isaiah 24:22, "And they shall be gathered together, *as* prisoners are gathered in the pit, and shall be shut up in the prison, and after many days shall they be visited."

Zechariah 9:11, "As for thee also, by the blood of thy covenant **I have sent forth thy prisoners out of the pit** wherein *is* **no water**." (emphasis added).

Zechariah 9:12, "Turn you to the strong hold, ye prisoners of hope: even to day do I declare *that* I will render double unto thee."

Let us go back to Isaiah 44:28, "That saith of Cyrus, *He is* my shepherd, and shall perform all my pleasure: even saying to **Jerusalem**, Thou shalt be built; and **to the temple**, Thy foundation shall be laid [New Jerusalem]" (emphasis added).

Isaiah 45:1, "Thus saith the LORD to **his anointed**, to Cyrus, whose right hand I have holden, **to subdue nations** before him; and I will loose the loins of kings, to open before him the two leaved gates; and the gates shall not be shut" (emphasis added).

Kings, leaders, rulers, and emperors were given titles. The Roman rulers were given the title of Caesar. The Egyptian king was given the title of Pharaoh and the king of **Persia was given the title of Cyrus, which means anointed.**

Even though Cyrus is a heathen and doesn't know God, the Lord is saying that Cyrus is his anointed shepherd who will do his will and build or rebuild the city of Jerusalem and his temple. God himself will hold Cyrus's hand and subdue the nations before him. Kings will be set before Cyrus so that God will be able to make the kings free and productive and the two leaved gates will be opened. God will break in pieces the gates of brass and cut in sunder the bars of iron. God will do all of this for Israel's sake in order that the city and the temple will be built.

Cyrus is a type and a shadow of Jesus who was anointed by God and who is our great Shepherd. Jesus said that he came to do his Father's will and by dying on the cross shed his holy blood that set all the prisoners free from sin, sickness, and disease.

The gates of brass, brass represents judgment, and sin was judged at the cross. Therefore, those behind the gates of brass are the New Testament believers, who only see in part, prophesy in part, and have a word of knowledge in part. Anything that is in part is neither whole nor mature, and it is not complete. Therefore, you are in a prison house until you can completely see and understand, until you are mature and anointed of God to make the captives free.

The bars of iron, and iron represents the law because it is rigid and hard and the law is certainly hard. It takes Grace and mercy to make you free. Therefore, those in the Old Testament who followed God by faith were anointed to set the captives free by faith and obedience. Moses was anointed of God and brought the slaves out of Egypt. Joseph brought deliverance by faith to all of Egypt and to Jacob and his family from starvation. Elijah walked with God and performed mighty miracles until God took him to heaven.

The Jewish people were waiting for the Messiah to set them free and to establish the Kingdom of God. Those who came by faith to offer the sacrifice for their sins were considered righteous in God's eye, but many were trying to enter heaven by doing good works and were in bondage to the law, prisoners of the law.

Isaiah 24:22, "And they shall be gathered together, *as* prisoners are gathered in the pit, and shall be shut up in the prison, and **after many days shall they be visited**" (emphasis added).

Isaiah 42:22, "But this *is* a people robbed and spoiled; *they are* all of them snared in holes, and they are hid in prison houses: they are for a prey, and none delivereth; for a spoil, and none saith, Restore."

Isaiah 29:14, "Therefore, behold, I will proceed to do a marvellous work among this people, *even* a marvellous work and a wonder: for the wisdom of their wise *men* shall perish, and the understanding of their prudent *men* shall be hid."

Evelyn's Night Vision

In September of 1979, I had night visions wherein Adonai spoke to me. I saw a city in ruins from an earthquake I do not know or from a fire, I do not know. Within the streets of the dark city, I saw a young teenage girl. She was beautiful and a light was coming out of her eyes, but her hair was disheveled and her clothes dirty and torn. She looked dazed and confused as if she had been raped. I asked the Lord. "Who is she?" and Adonai answered me, "She is my church." I marveled at the sight then I noticed a rather tall and large pile of rubble and people were trapped underneath the chunks of cement and wood, some were dead and others were injured. Justin and I stretched our arms out and a light came out of our hands and touched the people, the dead came to life and the wounded were healed.

Then I continued to walk until I saw a beach where a group of people were worshipping God with their arms extended towards the heavens. A glorious light glowed out of their bodies. They shone like the sun. The light was not on them but was manifesting out of them. I asked the Lord, "Who are these people?" The Lord was silent. I looked back towards the city and fixed my eyes on the raped girl and asked the Lord, "But Lord if she is your church then, who are these people?" Then the vision left. I said out loud, "God, you are going to have to show me this in the Scriptures," and the Lord began to open up the hidden treasures of darkness and the riches of secret places to me from His word.

End of Vision.

The Spirit of God is drawing God's people. The bride is also calling them. They will come if they are thirsty. Are we the bride calling ourselves? No. Then who is this bride Revelation 21:9–10 speaks of? That is a topic we will examine later.

No physical price is paid to find God, only a desire and time in prayer are required for those who want a deep relationship with God. Are you thirsty? Come and drink freely. The water is the Word of God. It is free to those who are thirsty. God is telling us that we are to come closer and closer to the Lord as we drink more and more of His living water. This is the river of life. We need more and more life until we are totally filled with Jesus Christ, Himself. It is no longer I that live, but Jesus Christ that lives within me.

Isaiah 29:13, "Wherefore the Lord said, Forasmuch as this people draw near *me* with their mouth, and with their lips do honor me, but have removed **their heart far from me**, and their fear toward me is **taught by the precept of men**" (emphasis added).

These people are religious, but their **heart is far from God**. Men teach their precepts. Their teachings are what put fear in others rather than the presence of God. This is a prison. They are under the law as they try to be very religious rather than doing the law out of love for God.

John 14:21, "He that hath my commandments, and **keepeth** them, he it is **that loveth me**: and he that loveth me shall be loved of my Father, and I will love him, and will manifest myself to him" (emphasis added).

Men Using Salvation as a Weapon to Put Fear in Other People

Most all men wish to go to heaven. Using that fact is how salvation is used as a weapon to threaten others into doing men's desires. When your followers think leaders have the power to shut the heavens to them, they will follow their leaders.

Isaiah 45:20, "**Assemble yourselves and come; draw near together, ye *that are* escaped of the nations**: they have **no knowledge** that set up the wood of their graven image, and pray unto a god *that* cannot save" (emphasis added).

Even if you escape, you must be watchful, so you do not get trapped again. Who taught them to pray to idols, thinking they could save them? It is religious leaders which is the religious spirit of Babylon.

Psalm 73:28, "But *it is* good for **me to draw near to God**: I have put my **trust** in the Lord GOD, that I may declare all thy works" (emphasis added).

Our trust is not in a religion, a denomination, or a church system. Some saved immature people are in grade one, and some are more mature and are in grade two or six, and so on. They are all saved and, on their way to grade twelve, spiritually speaking. We must come out of the lower grade and emerge into a higher grade, a higher level. As you can see, we will need to come out many times before we get to grade twelve. We must start in grade one but then we go from grade one and into a more mature group, grade two. Let us **not stay** in the same grade for ten years. That is not normal.

Initially, we are immature, but we must grow and become mature. Normally we come out from one religious system and go into another for a closer and deeper relationship with Jesus. This is just like our natural body which needs to change and grow into a mature body. We must allow the Lord to be our spiritual leader and not some man-made denomination, religion, or individual. This is not rebellion but a true desire for more of God. Yes, we use the ministries that God has ordained to teach us, but we are not to be in a prison house. We must come to a place where we learn to cut our own meat, and God's Spirit will teach us all things.

CHAPTER 3

The Five-fold Ministry

The Need for the Five-fold Ministry

We "must **grow up**" spiritually. Most people in Christian churches have been hindered because the **leaders are limited and tied to what their denomination has dictated. They are restricted to their teachings, commandments, and laws. The leaders have refused to allow the work of the five-fold ministry** as described in the book of Ephesians. The leaders allow the pastors to function, but they deny the work of the other four appointed ministries. How can the present leaders say the other four ministries are not needed for today when Paul wrote concerning the five ministries working together? God Himself gave the church, the people of God, the five-fold ministry as we read in the following Scripture.

Ephesians 4:11–13, "And He [God] gave some apostles, and some, prophets; and some evangelist; and some pastors and teachers; **for the perfecting of the saints**, for the work of the ministry, for the edifying of the body of Christ: till [until] we all come in the unity of the faith, and of the knowledge of the Son of God, unto a **perfect** man, **unto the measure of the fullness of Christ**. That we be **no more children** tossed to and fro, and carried about with **every wind of doctrine**, [cults] by the **sleight of men**, and cunning craftiness, whereby they lie in wait to **deceive**, [to steal the souls of men]" (emphasis added).

The five ministries are mentioned in the same line as the pastor is mentioned. We need pastors, but we also need the entire five-fold ministry to fully grow up. We cannot grow up to maturity without them. We are to **grow up to the fullness of Jesus Christ**, which has not yet been attained as of today. Therefore, the five-fold ministry is still needed today.

The Pastors and Denominational Demands

It is like trying to build a perfect house, and at the same time, we tell the contractor that we do not want electricians, plumbers, and roofers to come around. But we want a perfect house. It will never happen, it cannot happen.

Nor will it happen within the religious houses that man is building in the name of God. Without the five-fold ministry, we are tossed to and fro, making so many denominations, so many religious groups, and cults. When the five-fold ministry is not functioning, there is usually no one to discern when **false doctrines are introduced**. There are many false doctrines that have been introduced, which is why we have so many religious groups and so many denominations that **bring confusion and chaos, which is called Babylon**. These many denominations or religions **control their people** again as Babylon did. These leaders force their followers to follow their beliefs.

The five-fold ministry should be in operation so there would be true unity in the one body of Jesus Christ. Children are easily deceived, but the mature have the knowledge and can discern. They are all needed **until** we become mature to the **fullness of Jesus Christ**. Discernment is needed along with the revelation of God to grow up. Without it, great confusion will continue to happen and get worse as we enter the time of the antichrist. Many will consequently die.

God's desire was **not to** keep you in a pew under someone else's ministry, under the lordship of one person for the next twenty years. You are to grow up so that you can mature and work in your own ministry. You will be held accountable as to what you have done with your God-ordained ministry, whatever it is. You do have a ministry, and you will be accountable for it on the day of judgment.

Some church groups have more than one of the five-fold ministries working in varying degrees, but all five are needed and functioning in fullness. Because the five-fold ministry is not in operation and is being denied to the people, **the "church leaders" and the denomination they are under are in "rebellion," and this is that wicked spirit of Babylon**. This is man ruling man. This is man ruling in the place of God.

If someone is **controlling you**, trying to keep you under their ministry, they are working under that controlling spirit of Babylon. The spirit of Babylon is why we have religious prison houses that keep us in bondage in various groups. When there are no anointed ministers, the people stay in prison houses of their sins because of ignorance and no conviction from the Holy Ghost. Without the five-fold ministry, sin often stays hidden since no one is there to reveal it.

The people approve of this and stand up for their leaders as do children. The leaders, and thus the churches, are in rebellion against God's Word because they are exalting themselves saying, "We don't care what the Bible says or what God has instituted, we are going to decide for ourselves how to operate and how we should grow up spiritually." This is in rebellion to the Scriptures and is in rebellion against God and thus is Babylon as they sit on the thrones of their lives and the thrones of their organization, rather than God being the Lord. Still, the churches will not allow the five-fold ministry to work. God will move on. God will do a new thing with His people outside of the churches.

Ephesians 4:11–13, "And he gave some, apostles; and some, prophets; and some, evangelists; and some, pastors and teachers;

"For the perfecting of the saints, for the work of the ministry, for the edifying of the body of Christ:

"Till we all come in the unity of the faith, and of the knowledge of the Son of God, unto a perfect man, unto the measure of the stature of the fulness of Christ" (emphasis added).

First Corinthians 13:13 speaks of a better way which is love. Yes, but that does not eliminate the five ministries.

Love is serving one another and not domineering over one another. We are to love one another, submitting one to another and not lording it over one another. We are to lift one another as we pray for each other. Then there will be no divisions as the Word says. In the general church, there is to be neither male nor female, neither free nor bond, nor racial discrimination, for we are all one in the Lord. This is not done today. Try to say something in your church and see what will happen. You will be shut down and the door locked behind you.

Let us make each other free, free from any bondage or prison houses, free to come to God at any time, and anywhere. We are to be faithful to God, **trusting Him**, and growing up in Him to the fullness of Jesus Christ. We have to be one in the Lord, one body as God desires.

The five-fold ministry is needed to bring us into maturity, to learn how to flow in the spirit with power, and to learn how to discern so we will no longer be deceived, and the last days are the days of great deception. We need maturity in order to defeat our last enemy before the Lord can come back. Satan does not want the five-fold ministry to function, so he does everything he can to keep God's people deceived. The people are lied to as they are told they have all there is to spiritual maturity. That is why we are tossed to and fro by every wind of doctrine and then form so many groups to appease these doctrines.

God will yet have a mature people, and the defeat of Satan will be manifested. God still wants mature people He can call sons. We are His people and we have the privilege to become mature sons. Mature sons will be required in the end-times. You have been created for such a time as this, and that is for anyone who accepts Jesus and is born again in the spirit.

You are not to become religious. We are to become spiritual and mature. You are to have a love affair, a true relationship with Jesus Christ, **as a bride** who is infatuated and caught up with her bridegroom. She thinks of her bridegroom continually as Jesus continually did the will of the Father. Your minds are to be totally occupied with Him, longing for Him, waiting for Him. But our enemy is continually trying to bring someone or something else between you and God.

Anything or anyone, even if that is an anointed minister, that comes between you and **God, is idolatrous if that minister is idolized**. You're putting that minister in the place of God, which creates an idol and is idolatry. God calls it adultery because you are having a relationship with that idol instead of God, and that makes **you an adulterer**. This is against God, and it is not right. Therefore, we, individually and as a church of Jesus Christ, are to come to God and have a personal relationship with only Him. We are to honor those in the ministry, but we are not to set them up in the place of God.

John 12:24

In the Bible, **the church** is **referred to as a "woman"** who is to be intimate with only God and not idols. The church is to be in love with God, to be one with God, as Jesus was one with the Father as John 17:21–23 states. "That they all may be one; as thou, Father, *art* in me, and I in thee, that they also may be **one in us:** that the world may believe that thou hast sent me. And to love God is to love one another" (emphasis added).

Why do we have the hope of being able to grow up to the **same spiritual maturity as Jesus Christ**? The Bible says so.

Let us examine the story in John 12:24 where Jesus used the parable of a seed of corn that was planted in the ground. The plant grew, matured, and produced seeds. Jesus was the grain of corn (or wheat) that was planted in the ground. That grain of corn was put in the ground; it died but then gave life to a new plant as it grew. It **grew up,** and when it was mature, it produced **the same seed,** the exact seed as what was put in the ground. We are to become exactly like the corn that fell into the ground, and that is Jesus.

Jesus was put in the ground and He will reproduce sons who are exactly like Him before this is all over. He was the **first fruit,** and when you speak of "first," you are saying **others are to follow**. He was the first fruit to follow the Father fully. He was the first to overcome sin and the devil. He is the first to be faithful to the end. He is the first to be raised from the dead when He overcame death. Therefore, others are also to follow and overcome all these weak areas in our lives with the help of the Spirit of God. **The mature harvest is not until the end of the season, or the end of times.**

This will only happen when the grain is mature when we are mature like Jesus Christ. We are to become like Jesus Christ, and **He is the Way**. We are to follow the Way. We are to be full of Jesus Christ, and He is in us. He has overcome all including death. There must be a group that will fulfill the prophecies of Acts 3:21, Matthew 22:44, and Hebrews 1:13 along with many other similar Scriptures.

Matthew 22:44, "The LORD said unto my Lord, **Sit thou on my right hand**, till I make thine enemies thy footstool?" (emphasis added).

Isaiah 45:11, "Thus saith the LORD, the Holy One of Israel, and his Maker, Ask me of things to come concerning **my sons**, [followers] and concerning the work of my hands command ye me" (emphasis added).

43

God desires to reveal Himself to those who hunger for Him and His kingdom. We are to grow up, to mature to the fullness of Jesus Christ, and to bring children into the kingdom of God. We must be able to spiritually nourish these children, to make disciples of them. That is not to train them in man-made rituals or to indoctrinate them into man-made organizations but to fill them with the Holy Spirit of God. Baptize or saturate them in the knowledge and understanding of knowing the Father, the Son, and the Holy Ghost.

The book of the Song of Solomon 8:8–10 speaks of a young woman who is spoken for. She can have children, but she has no breasts. She can have children, but she cannot nourish them. She is too immature. She cannot bring this child to maturity. This is the picture of most churches.

This is where the general church is spiritually. The church is bringing people forth, but she is not feeding them so they can grow up in truth. She lacks the revelation of being spiritually mature. **She cannot give what she does not have**. People are brought in, but because of the lack of vision for maturity and the full five-fold ministry of God, the people are not able to grow. She gives the followers rituals and programs rather than a deeper understanding of a relationship with Jesus Christ and of **being in the Spirit**. Yet Scriptures tell us we are to grow up to the fullness of Jesus Christ. **We must go on**, and some will.

We are to be pure, virgins, and that means not to be involved with the world and its idols. We are to be mature as a full-grown bride who will be faithful to the Lord. She can produce children for the Lord. Then we will be able to bring forth children, sons of God into full maturity to be faithful in the ways of God and then be adopted as Romans 8:15–16 says, "For ye have not received the **spirit of bondage** again to fear; but ye have received the **Spirit of adoption**, whereby we cry, Abba, Father, The Spirit itself beareth witness with our spirit, that **we are the children of God**" (emphasis added).

Children need to grow up and become mature adults. **Jesus is coming back to lay His head on a mature body**. He will **not come back** until He has a mature body to lay His head.

Luke 9:58, "And Jesus said unto him, Foxes have holes, and birds of the air *have* nests; but the Son of man hath not where to lay *his head*."

CHAPTER 4

Zion and Her Daughters

Who are the Daughters of Zion?

The Bible also says that we are daughters of Zion. How can we **be sons** and be referred to as daughters also? How does that apply to us?

In the Old Testament of the Bible, the prophet Micah makes the following statement: "Be in pain, and labor to bring forth, O **daughter of Zion**, like a woman in travail: for now shalt thou go forth out of the city, and thou shalt dwell in the field, and thou shalt **go even to Babylon**; there shalt thou be **delivered; there** the LORD shall redeem thee from the hand of thine enemies" (emphasis added).

Here, the meaning of *daughter* is an intimate gentle description of God's true people who are referred to as the daughter, a woman, His people. Zion is the dwelling place of God. We, as Christians, belong in Zion. Yes, God dwells in us, but He is omnipresent and is present elsewhere also. Most of us have experienced the presence of God in varying degrees as we have attended different worship services and in our personal prayer life. We all desire and wait for the day when we can be in the fullness of God. Some have experienced this.

The daughter does belong in Zion and not in man-made ritualistic organizations. God is calling his daughter to travail, to intercede with strong groaning, **to labor in order to come forth,** in order to be revealed. The daughter is told to leave the city, the city of God, the **place**

of safety, and go into the field. **The field is the place for the harvest**. In other words, God is sending His people into the fields of humanity in order to harvest the souls of people. We, as His laborers, are to bring a harvest of souls into God's kingdom.

The daughter is to have spiritual fruit and to bring people into salvation, into the kingdom of God, but first, there must be strong intercession. In the field, she will be tested and **tried and there** she shall experience God's miracles as God delivers her. From the deliverance, she will **learn to hear and trust** God. **Tests and trials bring maturity**. Jesus learned obedience through suffering.

Hebrews 5:8, "Though he were a Son yet **learned he obedience** by the things which he suffered; [by and through tribulations He learned to trust the Father]" (emphasis added).

God takes His people, His daughters, who are truly saved, out into the fields which are in Babylon. Babylon is the confusion of humanity. Through hardships and much travail, God changes their thinking until they have the mind of Jesus Christ. He brings them unto Himself as they learn to hear, be faithful, and trust Him in all situations. He then truly becomes their Lord.

The fields are the fields of humanity that are ripe unto harvest. There the daughters will work and develop their own personal ministry as they work from the spiritual realm and not the natural realm. God will send them into Babylon, the world, and while in Babylon, they will be delivered from man's ways. They will be delivered from religion and from themselves. They will see God work through them as they see their ministry develop into full maturity. They will bring in a great harvest of souls into the kingdom of God as is prophesied in Scripture. Yes, many have been prevented up to this time from entering full maturity. But a new move of God is happening and many souls will have the veil removed from their eyes and will come in. God by then will have mature people to feed these new believers even during the times of their tribulations.

Isaiah 25:7, "And he will destroy in this mountain [religious mountains] the face of the covering **cast over all** people, and the **vail** that is spread **over all nations**" (emphasis added).

Yes, the daughters of Zion will be delivered as they give birth to their individual ministry and as they bring others into the kingdom of God. They will be delivered as they work the **supernatural works** of the Lord as Jesus did.

John 14:12, "Verily, verily, I say unto you, He that believeth on me, **the works that I do shall he do also**; and greater *works* than these shall he do; because I go unto my Father" (emphasis added).

There in the fields of Babylon, their enemies will see God mightily work through them. Her enemies, who have put her down, hindered her, who have stopped the five-fold ministry, and who even said there was no God or are into idol worship shall be stopped. Those who have said the daughters have no anointing and no godly power will now be silenced. The Lord will be faithful to deliver them if they first have **strong intercession**. They will see the fulfillment of God's Word and their God-ordained work as they **totally trust the Lord**. Great faith will be needed. They will have no other choice. They will be hot for the Lord or spewed out.

The daughters will go through tests and trials while in Babylon while sharing the Gospel with unbelievers. They will receive persecution even unto death, but they will also see the hand of God deliver them. They are delivered from their immaturity and thereby deliver their souls from the hand of man and the Antichrist even if they have to die.

There in Babylon, they shall see God work a work through them that has **never been done before**. This will be a new move of God. They will mature and be delivered so they can enter into their proper position in Zion. They will be called **Overcomers**. They will overcome Babylon, fear, sin, and themself. They will bring a great harvest depicted by the rider on a white horse, the first of four horses in the Book of Revelation chapter 6 verse 2.

Revelation 6:2, "And I saw, and behold a white horse: and he that sat on him had a bow; and a crown was given unto him: and he went forth conquering, and to conquer."

We see, in the book of Daniel, God who sent men into Babylon like the three Hebrew children Shadrach, Meshach, and Abednego who saw the hand of God deliver them out of the fiery furnace in Daniel 3:12–30. Through their obedience to God, all the nations learned of the only true God as Nebuchadnezzar declared to the people.

Daniel 3:29, "Therefore I make a decree, That every people, nation, and language, which speak anything amiss **against the God** of Shadrach, Meshach, and Abednego, shall be cut in pieces, and their houses shall be made a dunghill: because there is no other God that can deliver after this sort" (emphasis added).

You can be assured that everyone wanted to know who the God of these young men was so they would not be destroyed. God was thereby made known to all people.

In the book of Genesis chapter 37 to chapter 40, we see Joseph, the son of Jacob, who again was **matured in his test and trials**. His brothers mistreated him and even sold him as a slave. Later, in Egypt, and Egypt represents the world, the unsaved, **Babylon**. Joseph while in Egypt was initially abused again, lied about, and sent to prison because he did not want to sin. While in prison, he is given the charge of the prisoners. There he practices his godly spiritual gift of interpreting dreams. He also had to forgive all those who had offended him. God kept giving him favor, raising him up. **His heart was changing as he took on the nature of God**.

Because of his spiritual gift, his ministry which he practiced, he is delivered and made second in command to Pharaoh. He is then used by the Lord to deliver from the famine the souls of many people, including his brethren, the Israelites. In the end, he affected not only Egypt but also all the nations including the Promised Land where his brethren came from.

Verse 11 of Micah 4 goes on to say, "Now also many nations are gathered against thee, that say, let her be defiled, and let **our eye look upon Zion**" (emphasis added).

God's sanctuary is defiled when an unbeliever enters the presence of God or when a believer enjoys his sins. Babylon is the world as a whole where men control most everything without God. They, the unsaved and the religious, do not think God has anything to do with their activities. They do not think God's people are anything special. Now they are coming against the people of the Lord, trying to defile them by their actions and their words, persecuting them. Trying to force them into ungodly ways.

The Babylonian world will one day see why God's people, as Zion, the dwelling place of God, are different. Babylon will want to know why God's people have supernatural power and authority and they do not.

Those in Babylon will ask, "Why is God **supernaturally meeting their needs with signs and wonders**?" God's people will be a great hindrance to the wicked who desire to control the world. This will be especially true during the last day trials of the great tribulation which the earth will go through. The unsaved will be curious as they see the people of the Lord work miracles. They will come to look at God's people, not realizing that it is God doing it through them. God is causing this curiosity for His purpose, and that is to draw them to hear the Gospel and experience His presence and be saved. The unsaved will then realize they need to have God. Great numbers will come and accept the Lord as their Savior during this time. They will come because of their great natural needs and for their spiritual salvation and because God is calling them.

These unsaved people are coming to look out of curiosity. They do not realize it is God who is causing them to come. They come to God's people as Micah 4:12 tells us, "But they know not the thoughts of the LORD, neither understand they His counsel: for He shall gather them as the **sheaves** into the floor" (emphasis added).

Sheaves are gathered unto the threshing floor where they are beaten, the trials, and **harvested**. They are not to be thrown in the fire. The grain of the sheaves represents people whom God will bring into His kingdom, Zion. God's people will be harvesting these souls. In the natural, the harvest is done at the end of the season, and this great harvest is at the end of the season, the end of time, in the last days during a great tribulation. At the threshing, the beating of the sheaves is to separate the straw and chaff from the mature grain. The beating represents the tests and trials that are upon the earth at that time. The **harvesting of the grain** is the gathering or the salvation of **souls taken from Babylon** who are also after the souls of men (Revelation 18:13).

Revelation 18:10–13, "Standing afar off for the fear of her torment, saying, Alas, alas, that **great city Babylon, that mighty city**! for in one hour is thy judgment come.

"And the merchants of the earth shall weep and mourn over her; for no man buyeth their merchandise any more.

"And cinnamon, and odors, and ointments, and frankincense, and wine, and oil, and fine flour, and wheat, and beasts, and sheep, and horses, and chariots, and slaves, and **souls of men**" (emphasis added).

God will send His people into Babylon, into the world system, even during the tribulation times, to be changed by Babylon as Joseph was. There God's people will mature as they see God's miraculous work. She will again get the vision of God which is to overcome and to become like Jesus as they forsake the world. They will affect Babylon as souls are harvested and the immature church is fed by the Overcomers both **spiritually and physically** as Jesus fed those who followed Him.

The New Testament church brought their wealth to be shared with others out of **love** for the brethren. They lost the desire for the things of this world. The things of this world no longer meant anything to them. In the end-time the people will also bring their wealth unto the Lord to be shared. In the end, God will be the Lord of all His people and not just in a country in the Middle East or just one denomination.

Micah 4:13 says, "Arise and thresh, O **daughter of Zion**: for I will make thine **horn iron**, and I will make thy hoofs brass: and thou shalt **beat** in pieces **many people**: and I will **consecrate their gain** [grain] **unto the Lord,** and their substance unto the **Lord of the whole earth**" (emphasis added).

To be a "daughter" is implying that a mature woman is present and can thresh or get children. The daughter has to **come out of** the woman, and in this case, the **woman is the church system**. This is just like a child being naturally born. God recognizes the daughter that **came out** of the **church**. She will now arise and thresh or harvest humanity for their souls in a new way.

The daughter will now have power and authority. Power is depicted by the fact that she has a horn. A horn represents power, but the horn is made of iron. Iron was the strongest metal of those days and it could break any other material, depicting power and authority. Her hoofs are of brass. The hoofs depict the walk, and brass is understood to mean the never-failing grace of Jesus. **This is the great harvest, the reaping of the world, while Babylon is in full force upon the earth.** She brings the grain, the souls, into the granary. This is to bring the souls into the kingdom of God.

The souls that are saved are their gain and are consecrated to the Lord. The souls that are acquired will follow the Lord since the world is falling apart. **The kingdom of man is coming to its end**. These new believers will not get tied up with the things of this world anymore.

The daughter is now mature and is an Overcomer. The daughter's ministry, led by God, is to bring judgment on the earth as Elijah did against the prophets of Baal. Elijah was a prophet who stopped the rain as **he lived above the natural laws, walking in the Spirit, and not just the gift of the Spirit**. The daughter will have the spirit that was on Elijah, representing the **return of those works** which Elijah did **before** the great and dreadful day of the Lord. They will be the replica of Elijah. The dreadful day of the Lord is the day Jesus returns and judges the wicked. Elijah's work will be done before Jesus returns as Malachi 4:5 tell us.

Malachi 4:5, "Behold, I will send you Elijah the prophet before the coming of the great and dreadful day of the LORD."

Elijah also overcame death. The Bible confirms the work of the mature Christian includes overcoming death. This is victory over Babylon.

Matthew 22:44, "The LORD said unto my Lord, Sit thou on my right hand, till I make thine enemies thy footstool?"

The Overcomer's position is described in Revelation 2:26–27, "And he that **overcometh**, and keepeth my works **unto the end**, to him will I give **power over the nations**: And he shall rule them 'with a **rod of iron**;' as the vessels of a potter shall they be broken to shivers: even **as I [Jesus] received of my Father**" (emphasis added).

The book of Jeremiah also agrees with us. Jeremiah 51:33, "For thus saith the Lord of hosts, the God of Israel: The **daughter of Babylon** is like a **threshing floor**, it is time to **thresh her** yet a little while, and the **time of her** [**reaping souls out of her**] **harvest** shall come" (emphasis added).

The trials and tests are the threshing that is done by the beast and his systems at the end. The Antichrist and wicked men will bring the chaos that is going on in the earth. The chaos will cause earthly things to become worthless. The threshing will lose the grain; that is, **it will lose the people** from the **things of this world.** The things of this world are represented by the chaff. She will be made free from the sins that hold the woman and **her lust** for the things **of this world** that are a **trap and by man-made religious teachings**. The souls are held captive by the straw and chaff which are the things of the world, sin, man's weakness, man-made laws, and restrictions until it is. The grain is trapped until released. Then it will be free.

The straw and the chaff must be removed. The desire for the things of this world must be removed before you can reap the grain. During the threshing process of tribulation, the straw and the chaff that were initially allowed for her growth are now beaten and removed. The chaff is blown away by the wind of the Holy Ghost and the straw is taken out. Man-made religions, businesses, and organizations will now be worthless along with the things of this world. They were tolerated for the growth of the now mature grain but are no longer needed because maturity has been attained. The threshing or the beatings of the grain are the tests and trials to mature and teach us to **totally trust the Lord in all things**.

Isaiah 29:18, "And in that day shall the deaf hear the words of the book, and the eyes of the blind shall see out of obscurity, and out of darkness."

Isaiah's Scripture goes on to say this will be fulfilled simultaneously with the Scripture which refers to the **covering that is cast over all the nations that will be removed**.

Isaiah 25:7, "And he will destroy in this mountain the face of the **covering cast over all** people, and the vail that is spread over **all nations**" (emphasis added).

Isaiah 29:19–20, "The meek also shall increase *their* joy in the LORD, and the poor among men shall rejoice in the Holy One of Israel.

"For the **terrible one is brought to nought**, and the scorner is consumed, and all that watch for iniquity are cut off" (emphasis added).

When the veil is removed from our eyes, we can then clearly see. We can see the truth and are not deceived by the fine words of smooth talkers or charismatic men. You will now understand "as the deaf hear" and the "blind see" since you are not in darkness anymore. Now that you are no longer deceived and without any hindrance, you will have to make the decision to follow the Lord fully or to continue following man and be spewed out by the Lord.

As we continue to examine the work of the Lord that is yet to be fulfilled, let us look at Zechariah 2:4, which says, "And said unto him, Run, speak to this young man, saying, Jerusalem shall be inhabited as towns without walls for the multitude of men and cattle therein."

Jerusalem was the main worship center for the people of God in the Old Testament. It is used as a symbol here to emphasize that God's people **shall dwell in peace and security** in towns without walls and not cities. Cities are where man's glory of buildings and lights exist. These towns are in **no need of man's glory or walls** for protection. There is no need for walls for security, for God is their protection. There will be no more wars when God's overcomers reign with God. Mankind shall no longer be ruled by man.

Zechariah 2:5 goes on to say, "For I, saith the LORD, will be unto her **a wall of fire** round about, and will be the glory in the midst of her" (emphasis added).

God will be their safety as a wall of fire, and He will be their glory after He takes over and removes the Antichrist, the false prophet, and the wicked men that are His enemies. God Himself is the wall of the City of God, Zion, and He will be the glory in and on it.

Note that the antichrist is now free from the spirit of Satan. The Antichrist and False Prophet are sent to the Lake of Fire, and Satan is sent to the pit.

CHAPTER 5

Babylon and Her Daughters

The Woman that Represents Babylon

Revelation 14:8, "And there followed another angel, saying, Babylon is fallen, is fallen, that great city, because **she made all nations drink** of the wine of the **wrath of her fornication**" (emphasis added).

Revelation 18:20, "Rejoice over her, *thou* heaven, and *ye* holy apostles and prophets; for **God hath avenged you on her**" (emphasis added).

Her is referring to Babylon. Let us examine the word *Babylon.* Usually, when a woman is used, it is to symbolize the people of God, the church. In this case, Scripture uses Babylon as a symbol of an evil woman. **Babylon the woman represents being evil**, **the religious spirit, that influences and deceives mankind. It is in control of man's decisions and thus confusion deceiving her followers**. She represents all the man-made religions and organizations that oppose God's true ways and His lordship over every situation. Babylon speaks of religion where God is not ruling on the throne. They are not following God's ways. **God is not consulted or the decision-maker**. This applies **even to businesses** since the leaders make all the **decisions without consulting** or **hearing** from God. The leaders are on the throne of their life as was Adam when Eve was tempted.

In the Old Testament, we can see how Israel is referred to as a woman who is engaged to God but is unfaithful and seeks a relationship with idols and false gods; thereby, she is called an adulteress and a whore.

Jeremiah 3:8, "And I saw, when for all the causes whereby backsliding Israel committed **adultery** I had put **her** away, and **given her a bill of divorce**; yet her treacherous sister Judah feared not, but went and played the harlot also" (emphasis added).

Her is referring to a woman who represented Israel at this time because she is going after false religions of idols.

Jeremiah 3:9, "And it came to pass through the lightness of her whoredom, that she defiled the land, and committed adultery with stones and with stocks."

Israel went away from God and worshipped idols made of stone which represented animal gods or other earthly or heavenly creatures. It is easy to see that Israel was considered to be an unfaithful woman who **chose to worship other man-made gods other than the only true God.** These new gods became Israel's new gods. These new gods where the woman Israel was having an affair with and not being faithful to God. She influenced Israel's way of worship. This woman is this Babylonian spirit in man doing what he wants and not what God requires. This is the work of this spirit from Adam until the end of the book of Revelation.

Daughters of Babylon

While God speaks of having daughters, Babylon also has daughters. In Revelation 17:5 it says Babylon is a mother, and to be a mother, you must have children. **Her daughters are man's various businesses and the many religious groups** in the world. These groups **deceive** the people within them. There are many, and they all do the bidding of the mother, which puts people in prison houses and ultimately steals the souls of men who are trapped in them. This woman is wicked and demonically inspired. They have the spirit of Babylon.

Babylon and her daughters will fall as we see in Revelation 17:16, "And the ten horns which thou sawist upon the beast, these **shall hate the whore, [Babylon] and shall make her desolate and naked**, and shall **eat her flesh, and burn her with fire**" (emphasis added).

They, the kings, will hate the whore because she controls and has a greate influence on the people.

All the man-made religions of the world will **eventually fall**, including all denominations for they are **all man-made and have denied the lordship of Jesus**. This Scripture will be manifested especially when the Antichrist reigns. He will want to be exalted as God and will **persecute all that is worshipped** and everyone who seeks God. Everyone who does not obey his will, will be tried and perhaps killed if they do not conform. He will not allow any place in anyone's heart for God or even false gods since he wants to be exalted as God. This is the same deception as the serpent told Adam and Eve of being exalted as God.

Genesis 3:5, "For God doth know that in the day ye eat thereof, then your eyes shall be opened, and **ye shall be as gods**, knowing good and evil."

God is not interested in man-made religions. **He is interested in having a relationship with each individual**.

Let us now continue in the book of Revelation and see what God has to say about the **woman "as Babylon."** Keep in mind that God blesses those who follow Him, and those who do not follow Him, do not have His favor.

Revelation 14:8, "And there followed another angel, saying, **Babylon is fallen**, is fallen, that great city, because **she made all nations drink** of the wine of the **wrath of her fornication**" (emphasis added).

Here we see that Babylon has fallen. Whatever Babylon represents will fall and come to an end. **All nations have drunk of her**, and religion has done that. She is everywhere and has manipulated mankind throughout time. The control she has over all nations is represented by the nation's drinking of her wine, her will. Her manipulations are in all sectors of man's businesses and in religion stealing the followers of these religions and their souls. When she falls and is exposed, all nations will suffer in the natural realm, and the favor of God will be removed. Then the wrath of God will come upon His enemies. God's wrath comes on the nations because of their idolatry and the work of their own hands as they glorify man and not God. Judgment comes to them because God was not their Lord in their decision-making. Greed, power, control, and corruption are usually man's motives in this natural realm. Their decisions did not come from the Lord nor did they have a desire to know the Lord Jesus. Nor did they care for their fellowman.

Zechariah 4:7 "Deliver thyself, O Zion, that dwellest with the daughter of Babylon."

God's people are also referred to as Zion since God dwells in them. This is speaking to individuals who are destined for the city of God, New

Jerusalem. **God's people should desire to be delivered from sin, the lust of this world's systems, man-made religions, man's greed, man's control, man-made denominations, power, fame and seek the Lord.**

They are to be delivered even from man-controlled businesses as men make **business decisions as they sit on the throne** of their life instead of God. Since the business leaders are on God's throne it thus becomes religion. They must be delivered even if is hard to stop believing and doing what we have done all our lives.

The Babylonian spirit has touched every nation and every person of the world. That spirit has had an influence over every person, and every city, and has caused every nation to commit fornication against God as men sit on God's throne. The sin of fornication has been committed because the people of these nations have been introduced to false gods and are having an **intimate relationship** with those gods. These gods are **exalted by men who have lifted them up** in their businesses and in some cases are idolizing themselves. They are having a spiritual relationship with a false god rather than having a relationship with the only true living God.

Businesses do not consult God as they make decisions on their various ventures, making themselves gods sitting on the throne, rather than God being on the throne, being their Lord and decision-maker.

Revelation 16:19, "And the great city [Jerusalem] was divided into **three parts**, and the **cities of the nations fell:** and great Babylon came in remembrance before God, to give unto her the cup of the wine of the fierceness of his wrath" (emphasis added).

The city of Babylon is the representation of the **totality** of man-made religions and businesses that are in every city. Cities are the works of men, their businesses, and their cultures with their economic and social components, and with **their man-made glory**. This man-made glory is the glory that Satan offered Jesus when Jesus was tempted after His baptism.

Therefore, when we speak of all the cities of the world falling, it is a result of them following the Babylonian spirit. All the cities of the nations fell. **This is the fall of all man-made kingdoms, including their businesses, their governments, and their religions** to bring them to their end. It is not speaking of only the religious groups. It is time for the wrath of God to come upon them. God's wrath has come upon all of them because Babylon has a great influence on the people of the world. **This wrath of God that is coming is the wrath** that **God's people are**

not appointed to. The wrath of God comes when He returns.

Before Jesus returns, His mature people will have access to the spirit realm. They will be spiritually caught up with Jesus and miraculously protected during the Tribulation unless they willingly lay their life down. This is before the wrath of God is released on the earth.

That is why you are to come out of Babylon. That is the world systems. Let God be your Lord in all decision-making. Do not be your own God.

Revelation 17:6, "And I saw the **woman drunken with the blood of the saints**, and with the **blood of the martyrs of Jesus**: and when I saw her, I wondered with great admiration" (emphasis added).

Let us recap some of what we have covered. Who was the first one to shed the blood of the saints? It was Cain. Later, according to Scripture, we read of the Jewish people of the Old Testament who killed the prophets of God. Then it was Rome in their (un)holy wars, and now it is the Muslims, the Hindus, the Sheiks, and many others. Satan is after the souls of men and could care less what party does the killing.

In other words, Babylon or religion is man-made groups that are involved with religion even in their businesses. They are all the man-made religions of the world. They oppose the truths of God, using mankind's influences along with its military-political power to exercise Babylon's will upon other men. These false religions will even kill other men for not following them. These include atheism which is a form of religion and also businesses that use religion or deny God's authority. Regular businesses are a form of religion because the leaders do not consult God in their decision-making. Thereby, man is on the throne, making decisions instead of God.

The fact that a man is on the throne instead of God exalts man to the place of God. Thereby, man has taken the place of God and this makes **man idolize himself as God.** This is idolatry and of the Babylonian spirit.

Some people start right in following the Lord, but later they backslide. When they are backslidden, they are on the throne of their life as they decide who and how to worship God. Others use their man-made rituals to oppose groups or individuals from going on to the full spiritual maturity of God. These backslidden Christians then participate with the woman, Babylon, instead of following God as they kill and hinder the true followers from going on spiritually.

Religion has always had its followers **kill others** who follow another denomination or another religion. Even God's true followers have been killed. Babylon has and will kill or martyr many saints who follow the Lord in the last days. The **Antichrist will be the ultimate of wickedness** as Babylon approaches her end.

Let us continue in Revelation and see where the woman is located as we read Revelation 17:9, "And here *is* the mind which hath wisdom. The **seven heads are seven mountains**, on which the woman sitteth" (emphasis added).

The accepted spiritual meaning of seven, when seven is used as a symbol, means being full, **spiritual fullness**, or satisfied, **spiritual perfection**, or the total **spiritual** group involved being good or bad. Because of the context in Revelation 17:9, it is referring to the fullness or **maturity of spiritual wickedness** and of the totality of those who are to be involved. Seven in this case is a **symbolic number** and it is not necessarily the numerical number or quantity of seven. **Unfortunately, it is referring to evil heads, and heads represent leaders.** These leaders are **spiritually mature in evilness** in their wickedness. They are together as one. The woman is sitting on top of the heads. In other words, she is above them and controlling them.

Religion in Commercial Businesses

Seven heads are **seven mountains**. These heads are the **same as mountains**. The mountain is not referring to literal mountains as some would ascertain. A **mountain is the totality of any one organization** such as pyramid selling or any corporation. All organizations, religious organizations, business corporations, and governments have a head then a few more sub-leaders, and so on down the ladder. As we move down the ladder to lower levels of authority, more and more people are added to form a chain of command as in a pyramid setting. This is just like a pyramid, and a pyramid has a similar shape to a mountain. Putting all this together, we see that this is referring to the total amount of these spiritual heads, the evil leaders of these various organizations that are coming together and controlling all those below them. This is man ruling man. Again, this is not necessarily a numerical number of seven organizations.

We would be amazed if we really knew the amount of influence

Babylon has on us today. Jack Van Impe, an international television host who comments on world affairs, says 75 percent of financial businesses are into the metaphysical with a **psychic** on staff.

These business leaders are under that religious Babylonian power, that evil religious influence over them. She, the woman, "**sits on**" them **and controls them**. **Religion** is controlling and manipulating these organizations. If you study history, you will see that religion has always had a great influence on the world's leaders, even over kings, dictators, and governments, in their decision-making, even in their businesses and during all wars. Religious leaders were involved with funding some of the wars if not all.

During the **end-time period**, the Babylonian spirit will have a strong and great influence over the whole world, including the various religions that are over the whole world. This religious Babylon spirit says, "If you don't do what we tell you, we will throw you out and you will lose your job." Others would say, "We will excommunicate you," and by this, the religious implications are that you will not be able to go to heaven and you will go to hell. In some religions, the leaders simply kill you if you come against them. Some businesses and governments also do the same. The religious align themselves with evil leaders to push this wicked agenda as they threaten others by forcing them into labor camps if they do not comply.

Revelation 17:18, "And the woman which thou sawest is that great city, which **reigneth over the kings of the earth**" (emphasis added).

In this Scripture, the woman is the city. The city is the **totality** of what she consists of or is involved in, as in a city. But the city is the conglomeration of the things that men make which includes law enforcement, governments, religions, businesses, and other various groups. Here we are told that her influence extends not only to religious organizations but also to the rulers, businesses, and the kings of the earth. Through her various means, she influences businesses and most all leaders. This woman controls even the top leaders.

Since many leaders seek powers, they go into witchcraft to find greater supernatural powers as they fall under Babylon. Babylon controls them by saying she holds the **power** of heaven and hell. Sometimes she offers them supernatural knowledge and supernatural revelations which give them supernatural power and positions in their lives. In the military, they develop programs to enable their soldiers to have psychic ability to foreknow knowledge and to develop new weapons. These powers are demonic. In some cases, the military seeks supernatural powers and revelations on their enemy. They develop new more powerful weapons to kill more people and then Babylon can reap more souls. This is not of God.

God will also give His people information about His enemies to protect His faithful people.

Will Babylon Always Be in Control?

Revelation 18:2, "And he cried mightily with a strong voice, saying, **Babylon the great is fallen**, is fallen, and is become the habitation of devils, and the hold of every foul spirit, and **a cage [prison]** of every unclean and hateful bird" (emphasis added).

A day will come when God will no longer allow these evil religious spirits of Babylon to continue. There will be total destruction of all that is called Babylon, false religion, including religion in businesses. This will happen in all countries, regardless of the culture. Only the true God will stand and be in control. That will be the end of Babylon. This is the **end of man ruling man**. This is the **end of the Gentiles**, the unsaved which the book of Romans speaks of.

These religious groups, governments, and businesses are the habitation of devils and foul spirits because the leaders and followers seek **supernatural** powers instead of seeking God for their decision-making. They make all the decisions instead of consulting God. **They replace God with witchcraft or themselves**. Today's advertising, as you can see, uses sex and witchcraft to promote their product. The part of the business involved with witchcraft is religion, and thus, Babylon. This is very prevalent in the music and movie industries where performers sell their souls for fame and money.

God warns us **not** to be a part of Babylon or to partake of its powers as we read in Revelation 18:4, "And I heard another voice from heaven, saying, **come out of her**, my people, that ye be not partakers of her sins, and that **ye receive not of her plagues**" [the **wrath of God**] (emphasis added).

This "coming out" implies coming out of every man-made religion and man-made business of the world that men control. They will all fall and when they do you will be trapped with them if you are still a part of them. Will the Tribulation cause their fall to happen?

God wants all individuals to have a deep sincere relationship with Him personally. The Spirit of God will be poured out upon all flesh. He will reveal the truth to everyone including the present-day denominational churches that are in rebellion. Then they will have to decide as to whom they will follow, man or God.

The churches are in rebellion because they refuse to let the five-fold ministry of the apostle, prophet, evangelist, teacher, and pastor operate. This is God's appointed five-fold ministry which men have rejected as a whole. Most Christian denominations are in rebellion to the five-fold ministry and the working of the Holy Ghost.

The churches celebrate man-made feasts such as Halloween, Christmas, and Easter, while ignoring **God's Sabbath and His ordained feasts**, just to mention a few things.

We are to come out now because the Spirit of God is opening our eyes to the truth. We are to come out from those religious organizations that are full of man-made rituals and man-made commandments. In many cases, their leaders have no personal relationship with Jesus Christ. Some of these leaders consider ministering a job and not a ministry. When the pure truth is revealed, you must then make the decision to come out or to stay with man's ways. Many will come out but still some will stay in and will align themselves with the Antichrist.

You may say that your church allows you to have a personal relationship with Jesus Christ, so it must be okay. That is fine, but you need to go on. The whole Christian church has been hindered and needs to continue to grow up to full spiritual maturity. Christ himself said His people needed the apostle, the prophet, the evangelist, the teacher, and the pastor. Who are these leaders to deny what God has established? One day, God will have had enough of this rebellion, and His judgment will come upon the earth. Judgment will start at the house of God. God will and is doing a new thing.

Those who do not come out, their light will be put out as Revelation 18:23 says, "And the **light** of a candle shall **shine no more** at all in thee [religions, Babylon]; [no more presence of God, no more truths of God] and the voice of the bridegroom and of the bride [congregation] shall be heard no more at all in thee: for thy merchants [business] were the **great men** of the earth; for **by thy sorceries were all nations deceived**" (emphasis added).

This Scripture uses the word *light*, and light refers to true spiritual truths and life. They have come to a place where they no longer have true spiritual life and truth. The life of Babylon, the life of those religious groups will no longer exist. Revelation 2:5 says that if the church does not repent, God will take out their light, their candlestick from His presence. The life of that group will go out.

The bridegroom is Christ, but He is no longer preached or voiced in some organizations. The bride is symbolized by those who follow the Lord, but she is not heard of any more since there are no more true mature followers of the Lord in her organizations. There are no more people getting saved in her. The merchants are their followers who peddle the doctrines of those organizations and who fleece their followers. It can also apply to businesses that have no desire to make Jesus their Lord in their decision-making but are there to make money. Some churches are businesses.

Babylon is not satisfied with having **control over the nations**. She also kills those who do not want to follow her and are God's people.

Revelation 18:24, "And in her [*Babylon*] was found the blood of **prophets**, and of **saints**, and of **all that were slain upon the earth**" (emphasis added).

This Scripture mentions prophets who were killed by Babylon during the Old Testament period of time. Jesus said the wicked religious Jews killed the prophets. This again clearly shows us that all religions, including the backslidden Old Testament Jews, were part of this woman and not only the present-day church. The "saints" spoken of are from the New Testament period. "And **all** that **were slain**" confirms that Babylon was on the earth, even before Cain killed Abel, since **"all"** includes Abel, **until now**.

"All" includes those of the future, including those killed during the time of the Tribulation. She has and will have a great influence over the whole earth right until her end. Many people have been killed, just because the leaders of their nation went out to war for personal gain and not under God's direction. They sit on their throne position as they decide to have these wars. She will be judged for her influence in the killing of so many saints.

In Revelation 19:2, "For true and righteous are his judgments: for

he hath judged the great whore, which did corrupt **the earth** with her fornication, and hath **avenged the blood** of his servants at her hand" (emphasis added).

God will avenge the blood of His true servants who have been killed by the whore by her directions. God calls her a whore because of her many affairs with false idols and with other various forms of gods and idols which corrupt the people of the earth. God calls man-made religion a whore because man is having a relationship with a false god in a false way of worship which man has invented. They worship but not God's way. They do many various rituals that replace the true worship of God.

At one point Israel followed the heathen ways and started offering their infants to be burned to false gods. Abortion is a type of offering to false gods. God desires a true spiritual relationship with everyone, and that is not to be religious.

Here is an example. It is like reading a book and studying about your spouse but not having a relationship with your spouse. This does not establish a union. This will not make a relationship. God wants a true relationship. He will have every religion of the world destroyed which exalts man and not God. Then He alone will be the King of kings and Lord of lords. His way of worship shall be established including His feasts as the Scriptures say. His feasts shall be practiced during His Millenium reign.

We see God judge the great whore, treacherous Babylon. She is with and in mankind's various religions. She is with his man-made religions and their man-approved meaningless rituals which they call holy that have corrupted the world. They celebrate feasts that are not ordained of God such as Christmas, Easter, Halloween, and Sunday. The feasts they should know about, they do not do, such as the Sabbath, Passover, Pentecost, and the Feast of Tabernacles. Man-made feasts are not only in what is called Christian religions but are also in all the religions of the world. They have invented feasts and traditions for their false gods. They have no regard for the feasts which God Himself instituted and commanded them to be observed forever.

We see churches observe Easter, which was initially to the goddess Ishtar, and with sunrise services which are to the sun god. Then they have painted eggs and rabbit eggs which initially were to the goddess of fertility. Have you ever seen a rabbit lay an egg? They do such things without questioning their origin or logic.

At Christmas, we lie to our children as we tell them made-up stories of Santa Claus and stories on how and when Jesus was born instead of seeking out the truth. Then after lying to them, we want them to believe in the story of Jesus. The origin and time of Jesus' birth are totally man-made and contradict Jewish history. It is a story that was made up. Jesus was born in Bethlehem at an unknown verified time. Nor do we not know how many wise men were present amongst other things. He was not born in a stable but in a Succoth.

This is man desiring to lift himself up to the place of God and deciding what feasts to honor and how to observe them. This is true rebellion. Pray for discernment.

The fact is that the religious leaders and their rituals have taken the place of God and then received the exultation of their followers, is considered spiritual fornication in the eyes of God. The rituals **man has invented** and **called holy** have put a man in the place of God. The involvement with false gods can be seen in the Old Testament as well. This is the reason God divorced Israel in the Old Testament but then gave them a New Covenant.

God's feasts will yet be observed as we are told in Zechariah 14:16, "And it shall come to pass, *that* every one that is left **of all the nations** which came against Jerusalem shall even go up from year to year to worship the King, the LORD of hosts, and to **keep the feast of tabernacles**" (emphasis added).

CHAPTER 6

The Second Woman in Revelation Chapter 17

The Woman in Revelation Chapter 17

The Lord said He could not talk to His disciples of heavenly things, because their minds were on the things of the earth and they would not understand heavenly or spiritual things. The book of Revelation is a book of heavenly things.

Revelation means the revealing. It is the revealing of Jesus Christ and of His followers. God spoke in symbols to the author of Revelation, John, in order to relay what He wanted to say. We have to understand these symbols of which many are brought to light in this book. By examining various Scriptures, we can understand what God is saying in the book of Revelation. We have examined some of these symbols so we can understand chapter seventeen and some of chapters eighteen and nineteen of Revelation.

These three chapters refer to the end times, which is why they are **relevant to us**. The end-time is also known as a **period of deception** because Satan, the Dragon, is cast out from heaven to the earth. Babylon will be very active, desiring all the souls of men at this time. Deception will increase.

If we apply what we have previously covered, we will see how these Scriptures are coming to pass. Keep in mind that God refers to His people as being a "woman" but the counterpart of that is the seed of Satan, the **woman who is in Babylon**. Satan's seed is any creature, any person that is not of God and is consequently an antichrist but not the main Antichrist who will manifest in the temple of Israel.

Satan's deception continues in Revelation 12:9, which tells us, "And the great dragon was cast out, that old serpent, called **the Devil, and Satan**, which **deceiveth the whole world**: he was cast out **into the earth, and his angels** were cast out **with him**" (emphasis added).

This will be a period of time of great deception and confusion. People will be deceived by false visions, men's visions, false words, false miracles, false teachings. The miraculous will happen as a test to see if the people of God have discernment. If they don't, they will be distracted. They will lose the vision God has for a mature people. Those who are deceived will lose their souls to Satan if they reject the Lord and follow the Antichrist.

Matthew 24:24, "For there shall arise false Christs, and false prophets, and shall shew great signs and wonders; insomuch that, if *it were* possible, they shall deceive the very elect."

During this age of deception, Satan will do many false miracles, signs, and wonders. They will be manifested to deceive if it were possible, the very elect of God. Satan will try to copy the miracles Jesus did. Keep this in mind as we look at chapter 17 of the book of Revelation.

Chapter 17 starts by revealing to us where the great whore is sitting.

Revelation 17:1, "And there came one of the seven angels which had the seven vials, and talked with me, saying unto me, Come hither; I will shew unto thee the "judgment" of the great whore that **sitteth upon many waters**" (emphasis added).

The **great whore is the woman, Babylon**, who is religion in the various **religious systems** of the world and man-driven **businesses** of the world. The woman is the same as a spirit of religion or "religious systems" that influences the world since Adam and Eve. Adam and Eve made the first man-made religion of covering their sin by sewing fig leaves to hide their sin. Then there was Cain. He also made his own way of worshipping God.

Waters refers to the sea of humanity, the sea of people in these religions, and in this case, it means the people in religions of all the nations. The woman is **sitting on** these people, **on top of them! To sit on top of them is to be able to lord it over them and control them**.

Revelation 17:2, "With whom [the great whore] the **kings of the earth** have committed fornication, and the **inhabitants of the earth** have been made **drunk with the wine of her fornication**" (emphasis added).

The kings are the leaders of this earth. They have cooperated with this great deceptive whore. The kings with the whore control and manipulate the people. Most people are generally good and decent, but today people are deceived as if drunk. They have been duped by our school systems, false history, fake science, lies by our government, lies by the media, false books, false movies, wrong biblical teachings, false pastors, and more. The people are influenced and controlled by these deceptions which lead them into a sinful lifestyle. True spiritual maturity is nowhere to be found. The **public prefers their sins** rather than the truth. They believe in lesbianism, sex change, killing others of different faiths, abortions, false godly religion, and more. Unless a person seeks the truth, he will remain deceived and in a prison house.

A person has to become teachable and willing to change and accept the truth. Truth comes in prayer as a person personally seeks the true God while in prayer. One who seeks the truth will read the Bible which will confirm what the Spirit of God has revealed. Then a true relationship with God is developed. Otherwise, people will stay deceived. The Holy Ghost will teach you all things if you have fellowship with him.

The people of the earth are drunk, **drunk with the wine of her fornication**, which implies that the people are **not in their right mind** and are deceived. They are confused as to what the truth is due to deceptions of the whore, Babylon. Her religious systems and teachings in the whole world deceive those who are her followers. Even though the doctrines vary from religion to religion their followers believe everything they are taught by their leaders. Babylon is in all the world's religions.

The followers are out of their logical minds. They do not think for themselves as if they are fools and drunk. **Her wine is her teachings**, her form and way of life, and her beliefs which vary from religious group to religious group which she passes down to her followers.

Her fornication is the whore taking the place of God. Her follow-ers are having a relationship with her and her leaders. Various religious groups have their false gods. This Scripture is referring to Babylon hav-ing a relationship with all these people in their various false man-made systems of worship instead of letting the people have a true growing re-lationship with the only true God. **Babylon takes the place of God.** The people are saturated with her teachings. She is on top of them as she controls them, confusing them, and hindering them from **finding the true way** and of having deep and mature fellowship with God since they follow the whore Babylon.

Revelation 17:3, "So he [angel] carried me [John in Revelation] away **in the spirit** [translated] into the wilderness; and I saw a woman sit on a **scarlet** colored **beast**, full of **names of blasphemy** having **seven heads** and **ten horns**" (emphasis added).

John, who wrote the book of Revelation, is given a revelation of the woman. Being in the "spirit" speaks of religion. It is the area where religions are involved whether they are from God or not. It is another dimension different than the earthly dimension. She is taken into the wilderness. The wilderness is not where God normally resides.

Verse three tells us this woman, Babylon, has **many names** as she represents the many names of various religions of the world. She has **many names or many groups** she influences. Her many names take the names and the place of God and are blasphemy to God.

She is full of blasphemy. She is full of blasphemy because she has taken on **many names that exalt her** to the place and character of God. She does not regard or represent the true living God. She is nothing but man-made religious organizations and businesses that control mankind and are out to steal their souls. She is worshipped and has intimacy, a relationship with her followers as their god. They commit adultery with her. She sits on the beast. She is on top controlling or influencing them. To influence them they are guided by her instead of the Holy Spirit.

Who is the beast that Babylon rides on? Is it the Antichrist, the world's Elite, or perhaps the Satan? No, it is the **deceived people** within these various religious systems that give her power. The people allow her to ride them. Are they the serpent's seed that Genesis and Jesus spoke of? This is not an ordinary beast. **Without the people** within these various organizations, the whore would have no authority or power and would not be able to ride or control them if they didn't willingly submit to their leaders. Their followers will fight for her, even kill others who will not follow. By her words, she tries to sway God's followers into following her, if it is possible. The people are deceived and blind as if drunk and as all drunks do not see clearly.

It has been recorded that there are satanic ceremonies in which a woman, "Satan's Bride," has literal sexual intercourse with a demon while others watch. The woman is drunk or has been drugged before the ceremony.

There are also similar stories of individual women who have this kind of relationship with demonic spirits over an ongoing period. This whoredom may eventually cost them their souls.

The beast is scarlet in color, which is a blood-red color. Scarlet is used to identify the beast who has shed the blood of the saints that she has killed. This is religion against religion or businesses killing each other and against the true people of God.

She is full of **blasphemy** which again identifies her as being **against God**. Babylon speaks great words against God **as if she is holy**. The woman is lifted up in her own mind, but she is also deceived because she thinks her time will never end but it will.

Meanings in Numbers

In the Scriptures, numbers are very significant. Many nations consider numbers to be **not** only numerical but also have a spiritual meaning. We are using what we have learned concerning numbers and applying that meaning to get a biblical point of view of Revelation 17:3.

Let us see the meaning of the seven heads in verse three. Seven **is not** the quantity of seven but it could possibly be seven in number. It is most likely a **spiritual number**. The meaning of the number seven here refers to the **completely** evil spiritual **maturity** of the leaders involved. This is the **ultimate wickedness** which is full of spiritual evilness. It is the **evil maturity** of these leaders from these various groups. They could easily be many more than the physical number seven.

They will at some point in time establish **a one-world religious group** who have forsaken God. They will persecute God's true followers as they have done all through time. They will persecute and kill all the people who do not line up with their wicked thinking, even non-Christians. The people trust in their leader's teachings, doctrines, and denomination to save them rather than totally depend on Jesus's sacrifice. Their trust is not solely in the Lord.

The devil supports the woman because it desires to eliminate mankind and thinks it will then be able to **steal the** earth from man and break God's promise of giving the earth to mankind. This was the serpent's desire since the fall of Adam and Eve. This is why Satan tested Jesus after he had fasted for forty days.

Heads refer to leaders. The leaders of these organizations are very evil men who **give life or hope to the beast with their sweet talk**. Evil leaders have life because they have **followers**. Sin gives death to man, but life to evilness. These seven heads are unsaved men who are possessed, controlled, supported, and are **lifted up by the power of this beast** since it **carries** these heads. The seven heads have ten horns which are also carried by the beast.

Horn or Power

The horns in Revelation 17:3 represent the power they will be given. The number ten represents the **total complete amount of power** that they will be given in this natural realm regardless of how many or how much that is. It is the totality, the **total amount** involved, and not the quantity of ten. They will have all the supernatural power that is allotted to them to do their wickedness. Still, God is in control. God allows the amount of power given to accomplish His desires.

This number ten is not concerning spiritual things, but **physical** being the number ten. Ten is a **complete** number in this natural realm and after that, the numbers start over. It goes along with the "fullness" of spiritual evilness that these heads have and exercise in this natural realm.

Revelation 6:4, "And there went out another horse *that was* red: and *power* was **given** to him that sat thereon to **take peace** from the earth, and that they should **kill one another**: and there was given unto him a great sword" (emphasis added).

Revelation 6:8, "And I looked, and behold a pale horse: and his name that sat on him was **Death, and Hell followed** with him. And **power was**

given unto them over the fourth part (1/4) of the earth, to **kill** with sword, and with hunger, and with death, and with the beasts of the earth" (emphasis added).

A horn represents power. This group is not godly since it's full of names of blasphemy. They will have great power over the earth. Ten is the **complete allotted power** that will be given to these heads on this earth. This complete group is supported by the beast and is not of God. The religious leaders rule the horns since the **horns are on** the heads, therefore the heads control and move the horns as they manipulate this power. These men are in leadership being the heads. At this time, this last group of evil religious leaders will get all the appointed power that God allows them to have and from the beast they ride.

Let us continue with Revelation 17:4, "And the **woman** was arrayed in purple and scarlet color and decked with gold and precious stone and pearls having a golden cup in her hand **full** of **abominations and filthiness of her fornications**" (emphasis added).

Now Babylon, religion, the woman, has **exalted herself** being on top of the beast. To be arrayed is to be dressed in **what these vestments represent**. The color purple refers to **royalty**. Scarlet is the color of blood. Gold is for God, or deity. Stones and pearls are the wealth of the earth. This, as we will see later, is also confirmed in Revelation 18:16. Stones and pearls are also precious things or **secret revelations** and, in this case, it is for the secrets in witchcraft. They are used for incantations, potions, Pharmacia, and black magic against God and His followers. Religious leaders are supposed to be of God.

The blood of sacrificial victims in abortions, child sacrifice, and ceremonies of a black mass, are killings done by various groups and religions all in the name of their god which opens demonic gates. Satanism (Luciferians), various cults, and wars are all **open gates of hell.** These gates are in most countries which give access to the demonic to work lying wonders as it steals the souls of men.

The woman is exalted as a queen because she is dressed in purple, having power and authority. Purple is a royal kingly color. She is also dressed in scarlet. Again, we see the color scarlet as representing the blood of the prophets, the saints, and the people that she has killed under her direction **since the world began**. An example of this can be seen as we examine the exalted **spiritual** leaders during the days of Jesus. Jesus was crucified by the religious leaders and the Roman political system. We can also see this in the United Nations meetings as we observe those who speak. The UN is of this world and they wish to control everything.

Revelation 17:4 says the woman is decked in gold and holds a golden cup. Gold refers to a deity. Gold was also used in the Holy of Holies of God's temple. King Nebuchadnezzar was told that he was the head of gold as he **exalted himself** to the place of God (Daniel 7:38). Here we see the woman exalts herself to the place of God by her religious controlling actions. She is like Belshazzar, in the book of Daniel, who was exalted when he used the gold cup from God's Temple to drink wine with his women. He prematurely died for this.

She has a golden cup **in her hands**. The cup is symbolic of communion, the communion of wickedness, which she controls and in this case is in her hand. She has **in her hands** the power to control as if she is God. There is wickedness in all that she is and does. The cup is **full**; it has all that it can take. It is full of filth and abomination, full of that which offends God. She is full of abominations which she gives to her followers. She is full of evilness and wickedness as we shall see in verse seven. She has reached her maximum.

Revelation 17:6, "And I saw the woman **drunken with the blood of the saints**, and with the **blood of the martyrs of Jesus**. And when I saw her, I wondered with a great wonder" (emphasis added).

Wickedness has fully matured. The cup holds the wine, her life, the **life of her wickedness, and her killings** which she influences others to do. She offers the blood of others and gives them death.

She has reached her maturity as did the people of Babylon when they were building the Tower of Babel. God eventually had enough so He mixed their language and dispersed the workers. This stopped the building of the Tower.

Revelation 17:5 continues to describe this woman, "And **upon her forehead** was a name written, MYSTERY, BABYLON THE GREAT, THE MOTHER OF HARLOTS AND ABOMINATIONS OF THE EARTH" (emphasis added).

Note the words, "**upon her forehead**." Your forehead represents where you do your thinking. You can think evil thoughts, or you can have godly thoughts. Evil imaginations, evil inventions, and Pharmacia (drugs) that developed plagues such as Covid 19, mind control, or the

CERN experiments in Switzerland that try to enter into another dimension. All this is done to control mankind and ultimately to destroy God's creation as it steals their soul. Your mind is where you have the initial mark of the beast or the mark of God. It is what you think of doing.

Again, we see that she is against God since she is the mother of harlots and is an abomination on the **whole earth**.

Revelation 17:6, "And I saw the **woman drunken with the blood of the saints**, and with **the blood of the martyrs** of Jesus: and when I saw her, I wondered with great admiration". (emphasis added).

John was **not expecting** the woman to be drunk with the blood of the saints and the blood of the martyrs. This was beyond what he was expecting or could imagine. He had a totally different image of who this woman was since she represented religion. **This was a mystery** to him since religion was to draw people **to God** but this mother of harlots is taking them away from God and stealing the souls of God's people. God will eventually make a judgment on the woman.

Ezekiel 13:13–20, "Therefore thus saith the Lord GOD; I will even rend *it* with a stormy wind in my fury; and there shall be an overflowing shower in mine anger, and **great hailstones** in *my* fury to consume *it*.

"So will I break down the wall [your building, your organization] that ye have daubed with **untempered** *morter,* [not tested and not trusted] and bring it down to the ground, so that the foundation thereof shall be discovered, [false foundations, wrong teachings] and it shall fall, and ye shall be **consumed** in the midst thereof: and ye shall know that I *am* the LORD.

"Thus will I **accomplish my wrath upon the wall**, and upon them that have daubed it [teachings] with untempered *morter,* [proven truths] and will say unto you, The wall *is* no *more,* neither they that daubed it;

"*To wit,* the prophets of Israel which prophesy concerning Jerusalem, and which see **visions of peace** for her, and *there is* **no peace**, saith the Lord GOD.

"Likewise, thou son of man, set thy face against the daughters of thy people, which prophesy out of their **own heart**; and prophesy thou against them,

"And say, Thus saith the Lord GOD; **Woe to the** *women* that sew pillows (or amulets) to all armholes, and make **kerchiefs upon the head of every stature** [every age] to **hunt souls**! Will ye **hunt the souls of my people**, and will ye save the souls alive *that come* unto you?" (emphasis added).

Pillows were really charm bracelets that were worn on the wrist or arm to ward off evil. A kerchief or scarf was worn as a covering for protection.

Pastors are always asking who is your covering. God is the One who protects us. We are to be covered by the Holy Spirit of God.

Ezekiel 13:19–23, "And will ye **pollute me among my people** for handfuls of barley and for pieces of bread, [bribes, or for favor] to **slay the souls** that should not die, and to save the souls alive that should not live, by **your lying to my people that hear** *your* **lies?**

"Wherefore thus saith the Lord GOD; Behold, I *am* against your pillows, wherewith ye there **hunt the souls** to make *them* fly, and I will tear them from your arms, and will **let the souls go**, *even* the souls that **ye hunt** to make *them* fly.

"Your kerchiefs also will I tear, and **deliver my people** out of your hand, and they shall be **no more in your hand to be hunted**; and ye shall know that I *am* the LORD.

"Because **with lies ye have made the heart of the righteous sad**, [no hope for salvation or heaven] whom I have not made sad; and strengthened the hands of the wicked, that he should not return from his wicked way, **by promising him life**: [lies and false hope]

"Therefore ye shall see no more vanity, nor divine divinations: for **I will deliver my people out of your hand**: [out of prison houses, out of these organizations] and ye shall know that I *am* the LORD" (emphasis added).

This is the mystery of mysteries since it is so severe and for eternity.

CHAPTER 7

The Mystery Woman

Mystery Woman

Revelation 17:7–8, "And the angel said unto me, Wherefore didst thou marvel? I will tell thee the **mystery of the woman**, and of **the beast that carrieth her,** which hath the seven heads and ten horns. **The beast** [devil, Satan] that thou sawest was, and is not; [will not be] and shall [future] **ascend out of the bottomless pit**, and go into **perdition**: [later condemned] and they that dwell on the earth **shall wonder**, whose names were **not written** in the book of life from the **foundation of the world** when they behold the beast that was, and is not, and yet is" emphasis added).

The angel then explains to John the meaning of the woman, who is the beast and mentions the ones whose names are **not written** in the Book of Life.

The beast, we are told, was, is not, and shall at some point in time ascend out of the bottomless pit and then later be cast into perdition, which gives us an indication of it being destroyed. The only one mentioned going into the pit and being released later is Satan.

Who is it that their names are **not written** in the Book of Life? They must **not have been descendants of Adam** since all the descendants of Adam are written in the Book of Life **since** the **foundation of the world**. If the descendants of Adam do not follow the Lord, their names are **taken out** of the Book of Life.

Jesus had a new DNA since He was a new person from the Father. He was the second Adam, the second beginning. Jesus was made from or out of what the Father is made of, His virtue, His sustenance, and was not from Adam's created body. Adam was created from the ground but Jesus was not created as Adam was. He was from the Father's substance. That is why we can call **Jesus God** since He was comprised of what the Father was made of. Jesus was not from His mother Mary nor from Joseph. That is why we are special when Jesus adopts us and makes us part of who He is.

Revelation 17:7–8, show us that some of the people who are on the earth follow the woman but they will **stop following** the woman when Jesus returns and removes the Antichrist. After the thousand-year reign of Jesus, Satan will be loosed from the pit. He will come to tempt the people again to see who will follow him and who will not.

At the end of the thousand-year reign of Jesus, all the souls will come before God including those who sleep in the dust who have not risen upon Jesus' return to be judged. This is when all the people are released from death and from hell, for the judgement. This is the Great White Throne Judgement. In the end, they will all be sorted out. Some to be forever with the Lord and some will be cast into the Lake of Fire. After that Satan will be cast into perdition.

Perdition in the Strong Concordance is from a presumed derivative of G622; *ruin* or *loss* (physical, spiritual, or eternal): - damnable (-nation), destruction, die, perdition, X perish, pernicious ways, waste.

Perdition is what will eventually happen to the beast and to those who do not follow Jesus or have their names written in the Book of Life.

Again, in verse 7, we see God repeating and confirming Himself concerning the numbers seven and ten.

The woman is the demonic control in religion over people and the heads are the leaders of these man-made religious groups. The beast has or "supports, carries, lifts up, exalts" the seven heads and the woman. The seven heads are these unsaved, evil, demon-possessed spiritual **leaders** of various groups. They are **spiritual** leaders because there are "seven," and seven is the complete **spiritual number**. In the past, they have perverted mankind in various ways such as holy wars, introducing new man-made commandments such as female circumcision, and various ways of dressing just to name a few traditions that are all done in the name of God.

In the last days, they will do more wickedness on the earth than ever before. They will try to force a **one-world religion** upon everyone for a season. Their actions will be to unite the people, but the leaders have no real interest in God. Their agenda has nothing to do with God. Their agenda is to be able to control the public. They wish to control the public and reduce the population of the world in order to complete their agenda. This one-world religion will only last until the Antichrist wants to be **worshipped as God himself**.

The horns refer to power. The number ten means the complete amount or the **totality of power** they will have in this dimension for a certain period of time that is allotted to them and not the numerical quantity of ten.

An example of ten is "the full amount of power that a battery has." It is the **total amount** of power regardless of how much power the battery has.

Another example of this is of a young lady who said of the young man that he was a number ten. He was awesome to her taste. He was the fullness of what she admired.

Revelation 13:8, "And all that dwell upon the earth shall **worship him**, whose names are **not written in the book of life** of the Lamb slain **from the foundation of the** world" (emphasis added).

We are not to dwell on the earth and be earthly minded. We are to live in the spirit as the Spirit of God directs us.

Revelation 17:9, "And here *is* the mind which hath wisdom. The **seven heads** are **seven mountains**, **on which the woman sitteth**" (emphasis added).

Revelation 17:9 continues to tell us where the woman is sitting. She is sitting on seven or the total amount of **mountains** and mountains depict **man-made organizations** such as religious or business groups. The woman is "**sitting on**" the heads of this beast. These heads are not the same as the beast. **This beast is carrying and supporting these heads**, and this support allows the woman to exist.

This could be compared to a child who is being supported as the child goes to college.

"Sitting on" them implies that she is exalted above them and **controlling** them. She is controlling religion with their religious leaders. Their organizations are subtly controlled and influenced as she sits on peoples, multitudes, nations, and tongues. She is false in the fact that this is not what God established.

Revelation 17:15, "And he saith unto me, The **waters** which thou sawest, **where the whore** [the woman] sitteth, **are peoples**, and multitudes, and **nations**, and tongues" (emphasis added).

Revelation 12:9, "The huge **dragon** was hurled down. That ancient **serpent**, called the **Devil and Satan**, the deceiver of the **whole world**, was hurled down to the earth, **along with his angels**" (emphasis added).

He is cast down with his entities or followers to test mankind.

Babylon is a Mystery

Revelation 17:7–8 tells us **Babylon is a mystery**. Why? Why is she a mystery? Everyone usually thinks their religion will lead them to God, but does Babylon lead its followers to God? She, as a religion, is called a mystery because she is supposed to represent the true living God. She normally is in a location that men call holy such as a church, shrine, or temple. She is believed to be leading people to God. She is held up as being holy since she is religion. She is assumed to know the right way to spiritually live to find God and eternity. But the people get caught by her, and then she leads her followers into her ways, her deception, her wine, and away from God and into bondage, into **man-made rituals and sacrifices**, and ultimately **into hell**. She has stolen the vision of God from God's people. She does not have or give the vision of finding and becoming or attaining spiritual maturity. She is corrupt and full of deception, having her own agenda of destruction and **wanting the souls of men.**

She has hidden her true identity. Her true purpose is to hinder God's creation from finding the true way to God. She hides the truths from God's people from attaining the fullness of Jesus Christ that God has for His people which Ephesians 4:13 and John 17:21–23 speak of.

Ephesians 4:13, "Till we all come in the unity of the faith, and of the knowledge of the Son of God, unto a **perfect man**, unto the measure of the stature of the **fulness of Christ**" (emphasis added).

She desires the souls of all mankind. She does not want God's people to become mature because the mature people of God are **to restore all things** that Adam had before his fall as stated in Acts 3:21.

Acts 3:21, "Whom the heaven must receive until the times of **restitution of all things**, which God hath spoken by the mouth of all his holy prophets **since the world began**" (emphasis added).

Babylon is not satisfied with this evil deception and false worship. She also desires the souls of her followers. She also desires to be magnified up to the place of God. She is a **mystery because** no one expects to be **trapped and deceived by her** and taken to hell instead of heaven. She is supposed to be a good righteous religion. She deceives those who are religious, the lukewarm, and those who do not truly seek the truth with all their heart. She even tries to deceive those who truly know the Lord. A good lie is not black and white; it is ninety-nine percent true, so few can discern the lie correctly. She wishes God's creation to lust after the world. She wants them to be trapped by the things of this world that are worthless and of no value. The worldly activities are there to distract us away from God and from attaining His destiny for mankind.

God is calling Babylon, "The Mother of Harlots and abominations of the earth."

Babylon is a **mother,** and mother means she has conceived daughters, others like herself. The daughters are false religions that trap men into various false religions and cults. She is a mother because **man-made** religions have come up **all over the world** as they are led and supported by these evil men who are demon-possessed.

Sometimes the miraculous exists in these religious cults as they acquire power from the demonic realm to confuse the true miracles that come from God. Babylon causes her daughters to become like her, wicked and deceiving. She has many false cults, and false religious groups all over the earth as her daughters. She cares not how souls are gotten as long as she gets them.

Babylon's daughters are **harlots** because her followers are not faithful to God and are intimate with her idols and false gods. They are involved with false gods and false powers of witchcraft as they copy their mother. The daughters commit adultery and are full of abominations, full of witchcraft as these demons encourage them. All false religions cause their followers to commit adultery against the true living God. They have **a relationship with false gods** in their rituals and ceremonies. They recognize and honor other gods rather than the only true God in their traditions. In their dedication, they often kill others who are not of the same religion as they are.

They do this knowing or unknowingly. These people are led away from the correct ways of worshipping God, which God initially gave the

Jewish people through Adam and Moses. This **wrong relationship can also be with money, sports, status, businesses**, or other worldly treasures that are more important to an individual than God. God calls it adultery when someone is consumed by these things and is indirectly worshipped. They have a relationship with these things and not God. This is their **main focus** which preoccupies much of their thinking and time.

But the harlots are not satisfied with their adultery. This spirit is so evil that it will have those who follow her kill those who have a true love relationship with God. In the last days, any worship of **any god, any religion** will be forbidden since the beast will want to be worshipped as God. **This will cause the persecution of all religions of the earth**.

Daniel 11:37–38, "Neither **shall he** [Antichrist] **regard** the **God of his fathers**, [Jacob] nor the desire of women, nor regard **any god**: for he shall **magnify himself above all**. But in his estate shall he honor the **God of forces**: and a god whom his fathers knew not shall he honor with gold, and silver, and with precious stones, and pleasant things [treasures]" (emphasis added).

This Scripture is referring to an entity that will want to be worshiped as God. "Fathers" refers to the God of Abraham, Isaac, and Jacob who are regarded as the fathers of the Jewish religion. This entity has no desire for women which all men normally desire. The Antichrist cannot be from the Muslim religion since Muslims have a different god than the Christian religion's God and they desire women.

We are told this entity has no regard for "**his**" father's God therefore "his fathers" is a Jewish saying and is referring to Abraham, Isaac, and Jacob. He must be from the Jewish or Christian religion since they are the ones who know the "true God" of their fathers. He will not honor or care about his father's true God. And since he doesn't regard women may imply the fact that he will be a homosexual or will **not have any sexual desires such as being a robot**. He **honors** his god with material things but does **not worship** this god. He will regard the god of force which is the military complex. He will not honor any god since he will want to be exalted as God.

This creature is going to be unique. Later, we shall see this leader **evolve** from one thing into something that does not exist at this time. He is going to change from one character to another.

Will it come from science since they are trying to "create life" as God did and change man's DNA? Will his developers use gold, silver, precious stones, and treasures as part of this entity's makeup **as a humanoid or robot**? Will it be a draconian or a shapeshifter? It will not be a natural man. It will be demon-possessed.

The Mountains and the Woman

Again, we see Scripture repeating the number seven and the word *heads* in Revelation 17:9. It reads, "And here is the mind which hath wisdom. The **seven heads are seven mountains** *on* which the woman sitteth" (emphasis added).

Here we see the woman sitting on the seven heads or mountains. This cannot be literal. The seven mountains are kingdoms with their kings or dictators that have control over the people. Heads are leaders; these leaders with their **organizations are the mountains**. Mountains pertain to the whole organization of each individual leader. Each leader is on top or in control of his organization which is over many people, a mountain. This is not necessarily the numerical value of seven and **may be more or less in quantity**. The woman, that evil deceiving spirit, sits on **top of these leaders** and controls these mountains. The mountain consists of people also referred to as waters. The leaders of the mountains are being controlled by that wicked evil spirit to do her wicked work.

A mountain can refer to an organization or a company with its various levels of offices and authorities starting at the bottom with many involved and ending on top with one leader or president. There are many more people at the bottom of the organization with a decreasing amount of people as you get to the top, like a pyramid. This applies to all organizations. It can be a business corporation, a religious denomination, a government, or any man-made organization of any size, including your company.

The Woman and the Kings

Going back to Revelation, let us look at Revelation 17:10 as it says, "And there are **seven kings**, world leaders, five [5] have **fallen** and **one is** [who is the sixth] and the other [seventh] is **not yet** come; and when he cometh, he must continue a short space" (emphasis added).

Who is the sixth king? Who will be the seventh king or leader? Will he fulfill Daniel 11:37, "Neither shall he regard the **God of his fathers** [Abraham, Isaac, Jacob] nor the desire of women nor regard any god; for he shall **magnify himself above all** [above all religions and their gods, even Godly religion and God]" (emphasis added).

Second Thessalonians 2:4, "Who opposeth and **exalteth himself** above all that is called God, or that is worshipped; so that **he as God** sitteth in the temple of God, shewing himself that he is God" (emphasis added).

Five kings have been and have come to pass. There is one who was in place at the time of the writing being the **sixth**. After him will be the **seventh**. The seventh, no doubt, will be involved with demonic powers and become a different entity. The **seventh** will wait to receive power and then **he will become the eighth**. I assume he will become the eighth after he morphs into some other entity, into something or someone else. He will then get some supernatural power as he changes. Perhaps he will morph into some other creature. He will be different than any of the other prior kings. Perhaps he will be a new entity with no natural desires common to man. We are not sure as to what or who this character will become, but he will be different than anything we have ever seen in the past. He will only last a short time. Will he be the merging of man and machine or shall we say electronics?

To be exalted as God is religion, therefore we can say the woman will initially be involved with this process.

Revelation 17:11, "and the beast. That was, and is not, even he is the eighth, [will an evil spirit possess the seventh and then become the eight and is of the seven, [seventh leader] and goeth into perdition [ruin, loss, perish, die]. [At the end after the Millenium he will be cast into the Lake of Fire]" (emphasis added).

Daniel 11:32, "And such as do wickedly against the covenant [God's people] shall he [the eighth] **corrupt by flatteries**: [deceptions] but the **people that do know their God shall be strong and do *exploits*"** (emphasis added).

This creature will be a smooth talker doing signs and wonders. But the people of God who are mature and, on the earth, will discern by the Holy Ghost who he is. **God's people will do mighty things to show the works of God during this time.**

Six is the number of man or Satan's influence on man. Six plus six is man controlling man who is influenced by evil spirits. This will be **the end of man ruling man** as we know it today. God will allow all this chaos, wars, and confusion to bring man to his end.

Then will be the seventh. **The seventh entity** is a cunning, charismatic, smooth-talking entity at first but an evil spiritual leader who will become **mature in wickedness.** He will be given much power. **He will change, morph, into a new entity, and then be called the eighth**, the embodiment of wickedness.

1	2	3	4	5	6	7	>>8

Drawing: Six is the number of man. Man is in control with and because of his man-made armies. After the sixth comes the seventh who is then in place, as a man influenced by evil spirits. When the seventh is in place, he will change, morph into something else, and **become the eighth**. He will be given much power. Demon spirits will be in control as he is possessed. The eighth will become a **world leader**. He is the Antichrist. At the end of Jesus's thousand-year reign, Satan will be cast into the Lake of Fire.

A **fictional example** of this situation would be using a figure like Hitler. **He was and is not.** Some people think that he went to Antarctica and has not been seen. There in Antarctica he was cloned or **morphed.** Later, at some future time, he will reappear with power and authority.

This is an example of being the eighth, and later be judged and go into perdition, the Lake of Fire.

As the eighth, he will then do his work upon the earth where he will come against God's people, destroy man's kingdoms, and kill many. The eighth leader **is different** than the past six leaders since he has morphed into someone unique, the eighth. He has to be the seventh as he lived like the past six leaders. He lives incognito as an ordinary leader on the earth until he morphs into something else. He has to change before he can become the eighth. But only he becomes the eighth, and the number eight means a new beginning. Therefore, this is a "new beginning," but unfortunately, it is the beginning of a wicked period of time in which the beast with those who follow him rules with demonic powers in this natural realm. He will destroy and kill many. Only through the supernatural power of God will God's people survive. God will do many great miracles for His people during this time and through His people. They that do know their God shall do great and mighty things.

The Present-Day Beast, the Second Beast, and the Third Beast

We need to emphasize here that there are a number of beasts mentioned in Revelation. Some are good and some are wicked.

The first beast is in Revelation 13:1, "And I stood upon the sand of the sea, and saw **a beast** rise up out of the sea, [sea of humanity] having seven heads and ten horns, and upon his horns ten crowns, and upon his heads the name of blasphemy" (emphasis added).

The seven heads come from the water. They come from the **sea of humanity**. The seven heads are **leaders** of organizations, and or countries. They have crowns that tell us they are leaders. Again, seven is not used to show us the quantity of seven but that these leaders are involved with evil spirits since they have the name of blasphemy. We see these leaders are against the living God. The horns speak of power, and ten speaks of the **total amount of power** given to them, whatever that is, but only for a specific appointed time.

The heads have the name of blasphemy, telling us they are not of God and are wicked. Ten is the total amount involved regardless of the quantity. Ten is the total area or countries involved. Since there are only seven heads but ten crowns, we see that some heads will have more than others. The heads are exalted, even above God, which is why they have the name of blasphemy, and blasphemy is against God. Scripture tells us all men are *as* beasts. **The beast is a** wicked man or **a group of wicked men.**

The book of Daniel also speaks of beasts, and the **beasts are kings** or leaders of the earth.

Daniel 7:17, "These **great beasts**, [plural] which are four, *are* **four kings**, *which* shall **arise out of the earth**" (emphasis added).

These beasts are great. Four expresses that it encompasses the whole world—the north, south, east, and west. They come from the earth. They are kings or mighty leaders such as in religions or sections of the earth which they rule.

Revelation 13:2, "And **the beast** which I saw was like unto a leopard, and his feet were as *the feet* of a bear, and his mouth as the mouth of a lion: and the **dragon** [Satan] **gave him** [the beast] **his power**, and **his seat**, [one seat] and **great authority** [demonic powers]" (emphasis added).

The animals represent the different wicked characteristics this man or men will have. A leopard is swift and aggressive, a bear is ruthless, and a lion is strong and devours all.

Revelation 2:13 tells us where **Satan sits**, "I know thy works, and where thou dwellest, *even* where **Satan's seat** *is:* and thou holdest fast my name, and hast not denied my faith, even in those days wherein Antipas *was* my faithful martyr, **who was slain** among you, **where Satan dwelleth**" (emphasis added).

One interpretation to consider follows. Satan's seat is located in Pergamos, Turkey. Today it is a Muslim territory. Prophecy can have more than one interpretation, and perhaps this is speaking of a religion that is spreading across the world from the Middle East. They are being used to destroy many old demonic religious sites and Christian locations that are not of their beliefs.

God will put it in the heart of the Antichrist to destroy **all man-made religions**. Before this happens there will be a unity in world religions to form a one world religion which will consist of all or most of the world religions. Religion may be one of the groups these leaders will control.

This group is very much antichrist (Revelation 17:17). The Antichrist will eventually want to **destroy all religions** since he wants to be exalted as God and worshipped. God will put it in the Antichrist to destroy all the man-made religions because it is the end of man ruling man in religions. It is the end of men putting mankind in religious prison houses.

Revelation 17:17, "For **God hath put in their hearts** to fulfil **his will**, and to agree, and give their kingdom [the seven heads] unto the beast, **until the words of God shall be fulfilled**" (emphasis added).

Revelation 13:3, "And I saw **one of his heads** as it were wounded to death; and **his deadly wound** was healed: and all the world wondered after the beast" (emphasis added).

A Middle Eastern religion died to some degree in the past but is now revived. The world is wondering what is going to happen next. It was not an awesome wondering but a question of whether one would survive their philosophy should they get world dominance.

A second interpretation that is **very relevant for today** follows. The symbol of a beast being that it is a beast is not favorable. This beast has seven heads. Could some of these heads represent various groups of wicked men? Seven is the complete amount of wicked religious or political people. The beast comes from the water and water represents mankind or groups of people being from the sea of humanity. The group makes up "one" beast. One of these heads gets wounded. **The beast** has an agenda which is to destroy billions of people from the earth if not all. Could the **deadly wound** represent "**the desire**" of the beast for the great and complete **destruction of mankind?** But God will not allow it to happen and the head will be healed and not die?

Revelation 13:4, "And they **worshipped the dragon** [Satan] which **gave power unto the beast**: and they **worshipped the beast**, saying, Who *is* like unto the beast? Who is able to make war with him?" (emphasis added).

Who can wage war with those who are above the law and care less about what others think? The beast has no power of its own. It will get its power from the Dragon, Satan. Therefore, it is evil in nature.

Present-Day Beast

The present-day beast is religious and political. It represents a few intellectual elites who are controlling society. They enslave mankind as they manipulate the world through various means such as the media, monetary systems, and the control of teaching curriculums. Enslavement has slowly increased over the years with the goal of having total control over humanity with their ever-increasing laws, spying, and computer techniques. Then they will want to eliminate a great number of people with wars and bioweapons.

Using their position, they cause the "problem" and then have the solution beforehand, thereby being on both sides. This is very evident if one examines the wars of the world for the last one hundred-plus years.

We can see how the elite were the **money suppliers** to both sides of the wars. And, of course, they are involved with the manufacturing of the necessary arms and ammunition, and then the rebuilding of the destroyed property with loans. The loans would enslave the countries and the people who rebuild.

An example of this is the control of the oil industry and the shipping of oil. They are involved with the stock market as they knowingly milk the **stock market** with advanced knowledge and thereby enslave those poorer people who get involved with the stock market.

They control the types of **energy** we have and prevent any new energy sources from coming on the market. They have a monopoly, thereby they rob the public. They stop any new development of any new inventions that would hinder their cash cow. No one can interfere with their evil plot. They have exalted themselves above the law.

They are also involved with the **education** system to dumb down the public, keeping them busy with games instead of teaching students to think for themselves. They keep many students in dreamland drugs so they never learn, never think for themselves, and are easily controlled.

To help them steal the public's money, they have hindered the **medical field** as they stop the development of new healing medicines such as the healing of cancer. They are involved with the **pharmaceutical** industry where much money is garnered by selling unnecessary drugs to the public and keeping the prices ridiculously high. The drugs keep you going as they hide the problem rather the being a cure for the problem, not to mention their desire to put as many school children on drugs as possible. They develop new viruses to infect the public and then force the public to get vaccinated. Of course, they own the vaccine that is not effective.

Of course, you cannot leave **street drugs** out of the equation. You have in the past, the military to ensure the drugs keep flowing as was done during the Vietnam and Afghanistan wars. It now appears as if more opium is grown than was grown before the Afghan war started. All these street drugs have neutralized the younger generation.

They **control the food** industry through companies that develop various seeds and then control the seeds that every farmer must buy from them if they wish to plant a certain crop. These seeds are used all over the world, though some countries are now banning them. This is a means of collecting more money. This puts the farmer as a slave to them.

As they control humanity and the world's businesses, they are a beast. The beast gets its power from Satan in order to control the world. They do not function using only their own minds. We think of the beast as being **one person,** but perhaps it is **a group of people who are elite** in their minds. They have an antichrist spirit and care less for their fellow man. Satan is manipulating them and they are manipulating their branch of the world's population.

Amos 9:8, "Behold, the eyes of the Lord GOD *are* upon the **sinful kingdom** [elite's kingdom, man's kingdoms], and **I will destroy it** from off the face of the earth; saving that I will not utterly destroy the house of Jacob [God's people] saith the LORD" (emphasis added).

Revelation 11:17–18, "O Lord God Almighty…shouldest destroy them which destroy the earth."

We are already under a one-world governing power, **the elite,** who were not elected and work behind closed doors. They only get worse as time goes on. Their demands from the public are continually increasing. They will use crises that they created in order to control the public, which then enables them to reach their goals of being over the public. They wish to control everyone and everything such as gun control and population control in order to reduce the population and reduce any opposition. They will use the public to cause chaos and then imprison any and all who oppose their agenda as was done in Jesus' day and as was done during the 2020 Covid-19 crisis. God will eventually take action as He did in Babylon.

If you had an angry group of people, say **a million people,** on the street protesting and destroying everything in front of them, what could others do? Not much. I have seen for myself a similar situation in the Los Angeles riots. It is not pretty. They are full of hatred as they destroy and burn even things that their associates own. You really see the beast of man come out when they destroy everything, even their own fellow man's property. The police and the fire department could do nothing. They could do nothing until the rioters cooled off and went home.

These riots were due to racial problems that were motivated by demonic powers. Now add to the equation what the elite are trying to bring onto the scene of no food, no jobs, no money, no home, natural disasters happening, the economy is gone, plus now man's kingdoms are falling apart and wars are all around. The people are cold and hungry and famine is in the air. Then wonder, are these people fulfilling the description of **a beast**

and the desires of the beast being **beasts themselves**? There is no question they will be monstrous. Will this ugly beast be the beast that is mentioned in Scripture? Are we seeing the beasts arise in various countries today?

Who can stop these people with their elite leaders who desire to destroy as many people as possible? These wicked people spy on everyone and follow everyone wherever they go and track whatever they buy. Who is able to stop men who think they are doing the will of God or think they are gods and have an agenda to rule all the people? They are confident they will succeed. **This is similar to what the leaders thought as they were building the Tower of Babel.** Even God said that man could attain anything they wanted to do if God did not stop them. Do the elite have a desire to kill many people on the earth? Yes, but for some reason they have excluded themselves. Do they think God will continually stand by and let them continue their wicked actions? I do not believe so. No, God will come to a time when He will say enough is enough. They will not stop God's judgment regardless of what the false prophet prophesies.

Genesis 11:6, "And the LORD said, Behold, the people *is* one, and they have all one language; and this they begin to do: and now **nothing will be restrained from them**, which they have **imagined to do**" (emphasis added).

Revelation 9:18, "By these three was the third part of men killed, by the fire, [guns] and by the smoke, [disasters] and by the brimstone, [bombs] which issued **out of their mouths**" (emphasis added).

These disasters with many people dying are orchestrated by these elite who are under the direction of the Antichrist and Satan.

Revelation 13:5, "And there was given unto him {antichrist] a mouth speaking great things and blasphemies; and power was **given unto him** to continue **forty *and* two months**" (emphasis added).

The beast will operate for a specific amount of time that God will allow and no more than three and a half years or what it represents.

Revelation 12:12, "Therefore rejoice, *ye* heavens, and ye that dwell in them. Woe to the **inhabiters** of the **earth and of the sea**! for the devil is come down unto you, having great wrath, because he knoweth that he hath but a short time" (emphasis added).

Revelation 13:6, "And he opened his mouth in blasphemy against God, to blaspheme his name and his tabernacle, and them that dwell in heaven."

The Antichrist will blaspheme God, His tabernacle, even unto those who dwell in heaven. Unsaved people who are going through these hard times will curse God, commit suicide, and blame others even unto heaven for their hardship. They will even curse His tabernacle and those in heaven, the saints, and the two witnesses. They need to repent and turn to the Lord.

Revelation 13:7, "And it was given unto him [Beast and marked unsaved men who think they are God] to **make war with the saints**, and to **overcome them**: [testing and purification] and **power was given him** [antichrist] **over all** kindreds, and tongues, and nations" (emphasis added).

This is the great persecution of God's people. This will be a **time of being purified** as we totally lay down our flesh and **fully trust God**. This is when the saints will **truly forsake the world and the lust of the world** since they have no choice. But God will be doing great miracles during this time for His saints. This will be the sifting of the people to separate those who are cold, lukewarm, and those who are hot for the Lord.

Revelation 13:8, "And **all** that dwell upon the earth shall **worship him**, [antichrist] **whose** names are **not written in the book of life of the Lamb** slain from the foundation of the world" (emphasis added).

Revelation 13:9–10, "If any man have an ear, let him hear. He that leadeth into captivity shall go into captivity: he that **killeth** with the sword **must be killed** with the sword. [fighting with the power of the flesh] Here is the **patience and the faith of the saints**" (emphasis added).

These saints who are being purified will not, or shall I say **should not**, use any natural means to defend themselves, but to trust the Lord in all situations, as Jesus and the early church fathers did. They are to yield even unto death for a higher reward. The saints must trust the Lord who shall reward them accordingly.

The Second Beast

Revelation 13:11, "And I beheld **another beast** coming up **out of the earth**; and he had two horns **like a lamb** [charmer, gentle], and he spoke **as a** dragon [demon]" (emphasis added).

All men are made from the soil of the earth. This second beast is a man who is like any other man. He will get power from the devil. He is like a lamb and says to me he will try to imitate Yeshua, Jesus, who was the Lamb of God. He will speak softly but with power and authority as did Hitler. He speaks **"as a"** dragon, as Satan who is conniving and speaks with lies and deceit. As he speaks, he will be using witchcraft, causing supernatural things to happen as did the sorcerers of Pharaoh during the time of Moses. He will be the false prophet.

Revelation 13:12, "And he [false prophet] exerciseth all **the power** of the **first beast** [Antichrist] before him, and causeth the earth and them which dwell therein to worship the **first beast**, [antichrist] whose deadly wound was healed" (emphasis added).

This is a picture of the seventh king who has now become the eighth leader. The important thing here is not that he was the seventh but that Satan has now taken over this person. This is the personification of Satan. This is the reality of Satan. This is the **same spirit** that lost his kingdom because of Noah's flood, which was a deadly ordeal for him.

Satan tried to **steal the earth** from Adam and Eve and he still wants it. He wants a kingdom just like God has. That is why he deceived one-third of the angels. You need followers to have a kingdom. He deceived some of the angels from heaven who became the **fallen angels**. They also want a place to call their own, which is why they want to take over the earth. They need to destroy some or all of mankind. Maybe they will have a small group of people as their slaves. They will do whatever they have to do to attain their goal. They will not succeed and will be judged in the end.

At the time of Noah's flood, the fallen angels were altering the DNA of the animals and people. They manipulated the bodies of many different animals. This is when the fallen angels mated with the daughters of men and giants were born to them. The altered DNA changed all of those who were on the earth except for Noah, his family, and a few of the animals. God told Noah to make an ark. When the ark was finished, God chose the animals that went into the ark because God knew which ones had the right DNA since He created them. Then God caused a flood to cover the earth. All the people and the fallen angel's "creation" that were on the earth were destroyed. The **kingdom of Satan and the fallen angels** was destroyed. This was a preconceived plan to fight against what God had planned for the earth. Adam and Eve were given the earth. The fallen angels' actions were a satanic move. The flood that destroyed their kingdom was a mortal wound to their satanic evil plan. **Satan's plan in a sense was given a mortal wound**.

The fallen angels thought they had attained control of the earth at the time of Noah but God had a plan in mind they did not know of. All the fallen angel's creations with their altered DNA and the men were destroyed during the flood. The deadly wound that died was Satan's desire to eliminate or change mankind's DNA forever and take over the earth. It was to establish his own kingdom on the earth instead of God establishing His kingdom. The flood **was the deadly wound** since it stopped Satan and the fallen angels in their tracks. Their plan to change the DNA of those on the earth and to take over the earth was not successful. Satan's desire was destroyed. It was a mortal wound to him.

Scripture says Satan's deadly wound was healed and he revived. In the last days, **Satan will try again to revive his plan of taking over the earth**. This is the great healing of the wound. This time Satan is possessing or taking over the seventh leader who is now called the Antichrist. The Antichrist will try to take over the world again. This is when he will be revived from his fatal wound as he tries to take over the earth again.

The Antichrist will bring new ways to try and take over the world. Fallen angels will again manifest and perhaps demon-possessed AI will be used. This time wicked men will be added to his portfolio as weapons to control the earth. New man-made weapons will be used during the many wars as millions if not billions are killed. Even weather modification will be introduced to **cause chaos** and famines. Famines are happening because of these weather modifications that men have developed. These will bring many deaths. They will try to reduce the population so it will be easier to control and take over the earth.

Great weather changes will happen to **put fear in men** so they will willingly follow the Antichrist. The public will demand assistance from the leaders, which they will provide if you take their mark and worship the first beast called the Antichrist. They will try to rule the world through fear as they threaten everyone who does not want to follow their laws. But the beast will not succeed, and God's people will overcome as Jesus leads them. Jesus has hidden plans which He will put into place. Perhaps the Overcomers have something to do with this.

Today these evil men use vaccinations on all mankind in an attempt to change man's DNA and cause many to die. Scientists are working with man's DNA and even changing their intellect to be superhuman so men can be like God and live forever. Science is doing all it can to create new creatures, so they will think they are God as they merge man with animals and more.

After the great killing-off of mankind and peace is established will be "the healing of the great wound" when the Antichrist rules and reigns. The deadly wound was the desire to destroy man and take over the earth. Now Satan will think he has succeeded in taking over the earth. Through fear, most people will do what they are told. They will be told **they can evolve** into something great if they accept the mark of the beast, but **they will no longer be how they were created with the right DNA**. Many of the people will believe they can be a god and live forever.

Men will be easily deceived as they are dumbed down through religious indoctrination, demonic propaganda, and the educational system. In their minds, they will lift themselves up and self-worship. The **Babylonian Tower** was built to lift man to the place of God. Satan is still attempting to deceive mankind with his lies as when he told Adam and Eve they could be "as gods." Man will again be told they can be as God as were Adam and Eve when they were tempted in the Garden of Eden. The true people of God will discern this to be a lie and not take the mark.

Genesis 3:5 says, "For God doth know that in the day ye eat thereof, then your eyes shall be opened, and **ye shall be as gods**, knowing good and evil" (emphasis added).

Revelation 13:13, "And he [the second beast, the false prophet] doeth great wonders, so that he maketh **fire come down from heaven** on the earth in the **sight of men**" (emphasis added).

The beast, using demonic powers, will do great supernatural workings, even make fire come down from heaven to deceive those who have no discernment and who are not written in the Book of Life. Because of these miracles, men will believe the lie that the Antichrist is God. Perhaps at this time, the people who worship the beast will be given counterfeit gifts of power to duplicate the gifts of the Holy Ghost. This is similar to the magicians in Egypt who could imitate the first few miracles Moses did when he first entered Egypt.

Revelation 13:14, "And **deceiveth them** that dwell on the earth by *the means of* those **miracles** which he [false prophet] had power to do **in the sight of the beast**; [antichrist] saying to **them that dwell on the earth**, that **they should make an image** to the beast, which had the wound by a sword, and **did live**" (emphasis added).

Miracles speak of many miracles. The false prophet will do many great miracles to deceive the public. He will work in conjunction with the Antichrist who is the personification of Satan. God's people are going to need great discernment and be steadfast in following the Lord. They need **not be** moved by everything that appears to be **supernatural**.

One thought is that the people will be told **to make** their own image of the beast. This is **not an image given to them** of a beast. An unsaved man is as a beast. In other words, make an image of yourself and **worship that image, the image of self**. This is saying you are God. If you think you are God, of course, you will make an image of yourself as King Nebuchadnezzar did. The image could be a statue of the Antichrist as it literally says. This will be the worship of an idol in either case.

Second Peter 2:12 tells us unsaved men are like beasts, "But these, as natural brute beasts, made to be taken and destroyed, speak evil of the things that they understand not; and shall utterly perish in their own corruption."

The people who will accept the lie of the beast and make that their mindset will have the mind of the Antichrist and will **take the mark**. Then they will have that belief in their forehead. The forehead is where you believe and where you will receive the mark. Then they will put **their hand** to do wickedness. These people will be exalted in their minds and think they are God and will think nothing of killing babies in abortions, child sex, or child sacrifice, or killing others who think differently such as the saints of God. **Is not this the beast's nature?** This will be Babylon in the fullness of maturity. This will be the maturity of wickedness described as the evil woman who rides the beast in Revelation chapter eighteen.

Will they do miracles by the power of this evil spirit as God's people do miracles by the power of the Holy Ghost? Probably. This will be a counterfeit work again to try and void the works of God.

Today, scientists have developed an instrument, like a wristband, that can monitor your reaction as you see a picture or a person. It will record whether you like or dislike what you have just seen. It will speak to you or to others of your reaction to condemn or approve of your reactions. Your reaction will be recorded and you will be judged.

Revelation 13:15, "And he had power to give life unto the image [statue] **of the beast**, that the image [statue] of the beast should both **speak**, [false miracle] and cause that as many as would **not worship [as if he is God] the image** [statue] of the beast **should be killed**" (emphasis added).

96

The second beast had the power to give life to the statue. He had the power to give power to what the statue represented, even to kill. Perhaps the one who made the statue will then get the power to do supernatural acts. That person would be exalting himself as a god.

We have already been exposed to people having supernatural powers as we see in movies on television and in India. Why are they showing these movies? It is to condition the people. It is a brain adjustment before it is truly manifested on the earth. Those who do not want to follow and **do not worship themselves** or the Antichrist as God will be killed. Those who worship themselves and the Antichrist and deny **God's rightful position** will close the heavens to themselves. As they immerse themselves into this doctrine, God will remove Himself from them and give them a reprobate mind (Romans 1:28).

These miracles, these powers will convince these people they are on the right track and thereby reject the Lord Jesus as God. These deceiving powers will also convince others to follow them into thinking they are gods. These are **false prophets and false gods**.

Matthew 24:10–11, "And then shall many be offended, and shall betray one another, and shall hate one another.

"And many false prophets shall rise, and shall **deceive many**" (emphasis added).

Those who do not want to believe they are God and practice their own religion will be persecuted and possibly killed. Why? Because they will be reported. Or could the image which is the image of a man, or shall we say the image is **their neighbors,** who will report them to the authorities? The image is of man, and man, your neighbor, shall inform the authorities, and the authorities will take action and take you.

Mark 13:12, "Now the brother shall betray the brother to death, and the father the son; and children shall rise up against *their* parents, and shall cause them to **be put to death**" (emphasis added).

As we have ministered in other countries, we have already seen this to be true. Every neighbor watches their neighbor and constantly reports them to the authorities for any offense. Today, we not only have neighbors to worry about but are also constantly under surveillance via cameras on every building and many street corners, not to mention all the other monitoring being installed. Monitoring is done to the public via the Internet and cell phones, and many new ways are being developed.

The people will become beasts towards one another. Will there be any love for others in the last days as the love of many shall wax cold?

Matthew 24:12, "And because iniquity shall abound, the love of many shall wax cold."

Revelation 13:16, "And he **causeth all**, both small and great, rich and poor, free and bond, to receive a mark in their right hand, or in their foreheads" (emphasis added).

These deceptive evil powers will affect every sector of society. Regardless of their worldly status, these counterfeit powers will leave a mark in the forehead of everyone involved as they deny Yeshua's position and damn themselves to hell. People will be altered and brainwashed to believe their lies.

The mark is also on the hand because the hand is what you stretch forth to do good works or evil works, even of the supernatural. God does not mark the hand, because the hand represents the work of the flesh, and we are to do the will of God by the Spirit. God puts a mark only on the forehead since His people are to have the mind of Jesus Christ.

These evil powers will try to deceive the very elect if it were possible. Regardless of the supernatural, which a person might see, they shall know them by their fruit which is love. Love is to protect and defend one another and not betray one another.

Revelation 13:17, "And that **no man might buy or sell**, save he that had the mark, or the name of the beast, or the number of his name" (emphasis added).

The true followers of Jesus, Yeshua, who have not received some demonic mark or demonic supernatural power will not have ready access to buying or selling in the earthly natural realm. This is a way of forcing all to accept the beast's deceptive lies and to control everyone if possible. He will have anyone killed who will not follow them. The taking of the mark will test everyone to see if they are hot or cold for the Lord. The people will **be compelled** to decide and hopefully decide to follow the Lord.

Since all men must eat, it will be very difficult to resist the mark and stay faithful to God. God will **not forsake** His followers. The mature people of God will do the works of Jesus as prophesied, as they multiply the bread and fish to feed the people as Jesus did. This will drive many to become believers in Yeshua as they see and eat from the miracles God performs.

Revelation 13:18, "Here is wisdom. Let him that hath understanding count the number of **the beast**: for it **is the number of a man**; and his number *is* Six hundred threescore *and* six" (emphasis added).

Here we are told the number of **the beast** is the **number of man**. It is the **number of man** because the **beast is a man**. Therefore, the number of the beast is the number of men. Don't get distracted by the number 666. The issue here is that the number is the number of "man." He was a man before he morphed into this new entity as Antichrist.

Could this beast come from a UFO? No, the beast is not an alien, since we are told he is from the seventh who is a man like the prior six leaders or kings until he morphed or changed into the eighth leader. But there could be a false or real UFO invasion to instill fear in the public in order to control and gather the people to the elite's side. Remember these UFOs are demonic from a different dimension, the second heaven. Could a false flag be a man-made UFO invasion since men from many nations have developed UFOs? Yes, to instill fear in everyone. Ronald Reagan spoke of UFOs at a UN meeting when he was the president of the United States. Even if UFOs are from somewhere else, we must keep our eyes on the Lord as we **continue to trust in Him in all situations.**

Whatever the beasts represent, we must keep our eyes on Yeshua, Jesus, and totally trust in Him **for all and in all situations**.

The Third Manifestation of the Beast

There is another beast who opposes the Lord. This beast will come out of the bottomless pit.

Revelation 20:2–3 "And he laid hold on the **dragon**, that **old serpent**, which is the Devil, and Satan, and **bound him a thousand years,**

"And **cast him [Satan] into the bottomless pit**, and shut him up, and set a seal upon him, that he should deceive the nations no more, **till the thousand years should be fulfilled**: and after that he must be loosed a little season" (emphasis added).

The spirit of Satan has by now left the Antichrist. This beast, Satan who will oppose the Lord, is put into the pit. This beast will be released out of the bottomless pit towards the end of the thousand-year reign of Jesus. He will once again come to test the people on the earth.

Revelation 17:8, "**The beast** [Satan] that thou sawest was, and is not; [he is in the pit] and shall **ascend out** of the **bottomless pit**, [at the end of the thousand years] and [later, after the thousand years] go into **perdition:** [destruction] and they that dwell on the earth shall wonder, whose names were **not written** in the book of life **from the foundation of the world**, [written in the Book of Life when the foundation of the world was established] when they behold **the beast that was,** [during man ruling man, Old Testament and New Testament] and **is not, [Satan is sent to the Bottomless Pit] and yet is [release from the pit to test those on the earth at the end of the Thousand Year Millenium]**" (emphasis added).

This next statement is spoken as if in the future. The beast, Satan "that was," before he was put in the pit during the Tribulation. After the Tribulation, he is put into the pit. Towards the end of the thousand-year reign, he is released from the pit to test the people. The test will show who will remain faithful to the Lord Jesus and who will not.

When Jesus returns, Satan will be taken and **put in** the bottomless pit. He is **not put in** the Lake of Fire where the False Prophet and the Antichrist are sent at that time.In other words, he, Satan, is in existence now and will be sent to the bottomless pit when Jesus returns. He is released at the end of the thousand-year rule of Jesus to again test those who are on the earth.

After the thousand-year reign, Satan and his followers will battle with the Lord. Satan will gather those who oppose Jesus to fight Jesus and His followers. Satan's followers will be destroyed by the Lord's brightness and Satan will be put in the Lake of Fire (Revelation 20:10) with the False Prophet and the Beast.

"And the **devil** that deceived them was **cast into the lake of fire** and brimstone, where the **beast [antichrist] and the false prophet** are, and shall be tormented day and night for ever and ever" (emphasis added).

The Defeat of Satan

Revelation 20:7–10 "And when the **thousand years** are expired, **Satan shall be loosed** out of his prison, [from the Bottomless Pit]

"And shall go out **to deceive the nations** which are in the four quarters of the earth, Gog and Magog, to **gather them together to battle**: the number of whom is as the sand of the sea.

"And they went up on the breadth of the earth, and **compassed the camp of the saints** about, and the **beloved city: and fire came down from God out of heaven, and devoured them**.

"And the **devil** that deceived them was **cast into the lake of fire** and brimstone, where the **beast [antichrist] and the false prophet** are, and shall be tormented day and night for ever and ever" (emphasis added).

Satan and his followers are the ones who will come against Jesus to war with Jesus. The followers will be against God and will get their power from Satan, the beast, when he comes out from the pit. His followers will no doubt be demon-possessed, allowing them to have demonic power.

Revelation 17:14, "These shall make war with the Lamb, and the Lamb shall overcome them: for he is Lord of lords, and King of kings: and they that are with him *are* called, and chosen, and faithful."

Book of Life

Revelation 17:8, "The beast that thou sawest was, and is not; and shall ascend out of the bottomless pit, and go into perdition: and they that dwell on the earth shall wonder, **whose names were not written in the book of life from the foundation of the world,** when they behold the beast that was, and is not, and yet is" (emphasis added).

If you are born of man your name was put in the book of life when you were born. If you reject the Lord your name is **removed** from the book. According to the Scriptures some will not have their name written in the Book of Life at any time not even when they were born. Are they the tares the enemy lanted? It seems they are not from the seed of man. Those not written in the Book of Life will have a different DNA than those born as descendants of Adam and Eve. Those following the beast will have no discernment.

This beast that was and is not, yet is, is the same as the **eighth beast** that shall rule the world. Satan will possess the seventh and become the eighth. When he manifests, he is the last ruler. This beast is not like the other prior beasts. He will want to be **worshipped as God**. He shall kill the **Lord's two witnesses** along with **many of God's saints**. The saints who are on the earth will be able to observe this beast and renounce him as they stand firm for the Lord.

Two Witnesses

We need to consider what a covenant is. It is an agreement done and agreed by two or more parties. In the Old Testament, the word *testament* could read covenant. The Old Covenant was God through Moses making an agreement with the people who followed Moses, which included Israel and others. The covenant with its laws was a testimony of God and what He was doing. It was a witness of God. God was setting forth His foundation for His people. The Law and the Prophets are the foundation.

Revelation 11:3–7, "And **I [Jesus] will give** *power* **unto my two witnesses**, and they shall prophesy a thousand two hundred *and* threescore days, clothed in sackcloth **three and a half years.**

"**These are** [witnesses] the **two olive trees**, and the **two candlesticks** standing before the God of the earth" (emphasis added).

Revelation 1:20, "the mystery of the seven stars which thou sawest in my right hand, and the seven golden candlesticks. The seven **stars** are the **angels** of the seven churches: and the seven **candlesticks** are seven churches [people in the church are witnesses]" (emphasis added).

The two witnesses **are the two candlesticks** and **are also the two olive trees** standing before God. Who stands before God? The people of God in the church under the law of the Old Testament and the people under grace of the New Testament.

The two witnesses have been described as being the **Old Testament** and the **New Testament** because they testify of the Lord. The law has never failed to exist to this day. The Law is what makes sin, sin. Without the Law, there is no sin. The Law has never been done away with.

The people of the Old Covenant forsook the Law of God and went after other gods and idols. Then God divorced the people but the Law still existed because God is faithful to His Word. The Law was good and perfect, which Jesus fulfilled. He as a man did all the Law. The Law is the foundation for the true church, the kingdom of God.

Today, the New Testament of grace is alive and well but the people are leaving the churches that have no power. God's people are supposed to be a witness to the world as they work with **God's power**. The Bible is being altered and manipulated to justify and satisfy man's way of living as corruption increases. God will allow it for a season just as He did to the Old Testament, then He will take action. As you study my book, **Antichrist and the Third Day Overcomers** you see that **a third move of God** will follow the New Covenant. This may well be a very short period of time. God will not forsake His people who are faithful to Him and are Overcomers who will do the works of Jesus as they fulfill the Scriptures.

You have read by now how **God will give man-made religions to the Antichrist for their destruction. Then the people will leave their religious man-made systems all over the world.** You cannot be lawless nor can men negate the work of the cross that seals the New Covenant.

The Law has never been done away with nor will the covenant of the shed blood of Jesus. What people do does not negate what Jesus did on the cross.

The New Covenant is better than the Old Covenant. The new move of God of today brings the fulfillment and maturity of the believers. The three moves of God were planned from the foundation of the world. Jesus was crucified before the foundation of the world. Maturity brings the manifestation of the sons of God.

Romans 8:19, "For the earnest expectation of the creature waiteth for the manifestation of the sons of God."

The apostles and the prophets of the New Covenant build on the Law and Prophets of the Old Covenant. The manifestation of the glory of God over many parts of the earth at this time is proof we are moving into a third move of God that will bring spiritual maturity, the Overcomers of Revelation 2:26, "And he that **overcometh,** and keepeth my works unto the end, to him will I give power over the nations" (emphasis added). They will do the works of Jesus and greater works as the Scriptures tell us.

A New Move of God

Why a new move of God? Because the world religions have left His truths and **trusted** in man-made religious traditions rather than having a personal relationship with God. These religious people think by doing their rituals they will be forgiven of their sins and be saved. They are deceived and are in a prison house of their religious traditions. They do not have a true personal relationship with the living God. Some are totally anti-God as they worship evil spirits.

These Babylonian **religious systems** of the world along with businesses will be destroyed by the Antichrist. The Antichrist will force the people to leave their religions and their man-controlled businesses to come and worship Him and Satan.

But in reality, God knew the spiritual condition man was going to be in at this time and **He planned a new move of God from the beginning**.

For the first group of people, their way of salvation was the Law. The people followed the voice of Moses. The Law could make nothing perfect, according to Hebrews 7:19.

The second group's way of salvation was by making it possible to keep the Law by the shed blood of Jesus and the power of the Holy Spirit. The blood of Jesus provided salvation. These people follow the voice of Jesus.

Romans 8:2–5, **"For the law of the Spirit of life in Christ Jesus** made me free from the law of sin and of death.

"For what the law could not do, in that it was weak through the flesh, God, sending his own Son in the likeness of sinful flesh and *as an offering* for sin, condemned sin in the flesh:

"that the **ordinance** of the law might be **fulfilled in us**, who **walk not after the flesh, but after the spirit** [overcoming sin].

"For they that are after the flesh do mind the things of the flesh; but they **that are after the spirit the things of the spirit**" (emphasis added).

The third group of people are different. No one can understand what they have to say because they only speak the **language of Father God**. They belong to the Father. They follow the voice of the Father. This group follows Jesus wherever He goes at a time when the world will be in rebellion and in sin.

Revelation 14:3, "and they sing as it were a new song before the throne, and before the four living creatures and the elders: and no man could learn the song save the hundred and forty and four thousand, *even* they that had been purchased out of the earth."

During the time of this Antichrist evil control, God will not forsake His people. God's Overcomers will feed His immature people both spiritually and physically. This will be done now and during the tribulation.

The book of Revelation continues in chapter 11:4–7.

Revelation 11:4-7, "These are the two olive trees, and the two candlesticks standing before the God of the earth.

"And if any man will hurt them, fire proceedeth out of their mouth, and devoureth their enemies: and if any man will hurt them, he must in this manner be killed.

"These have power to shut heaven, that it rain not in the days of their prophecy: and have power over waters to turn them to blood, and to smite the earth with all plagues, as often as they will.

"And when they shall have finished their testimony, the beast that ascendeth out of the bottomless pit shall make war against them, and shall overcome them, and kill them".

The word that he "ascended" is used to identify who this beast is but he has not at this time been put into the pit. He has just now killed the two witnesses and at the end when Jesus returns, He will put Satan in the pit.

When two people appear as the two witnesses whom Revelation speaks of, they surely will testify of the power and truths of God. They will testify of the only true living God. They will try for three and a half years to force or compel the people to turn to God. After one thousand two hundred *and* threescore days (1260 days) the two witnesses will be killed by the **beast who will later come out of the bottomless pit**. The mention of the one who came out of the bottomless pit is to identify who that is and is not used as a sequence in time. The two witnesses will overcome death after three and a half days and be resurrected as will all the true people of God when the Lord returns. This event is before Jesus' return. This miraculous manifestation is to show the saints that they can also overcome death, their last enemy.

Some say the two witnesses are Moses and Elijah, but scripture says Moses did die. Why not Enoch? Why not a present-day saint?

Why Are the Two Witnesses Killed

God will allow the two witnesses to be killed **to bring unity** to the beast's followers. They will then say that the beast, Satan, is stronger than God; therefore, many will say yes to Satan, and will become his followers. The weak and lukewarm believers may also start to follow the beast due to the persecution and the miracles the Antichrist and Satan will do. But the Overcomers will be there to help the immature believers and encourage them to stay faithful to God and to keep their eyes on the Lord. The Overcomers will work the miraculous as did Jesus.

Daniel 11:32, "And such as do wickedly **against the covenant** [against the foundations of the Old and New Covenant] shall he corrupt by flatteries: but the people that do **know their God** shall be strong, and **do *exploits***" (emphasis added).

CHAPTER 8

Persecution

Persecution of the Righteous

The world's religions have, are, and will kill many of God's people along with other people, no doubt. Those who truly seek God will always be persecuted. Religion, **as Babylon**, sits **as a queen** since the Old Testament. She acts as a religious leader on both sides. She has taken the power to rule and kill as many people as she wants. She cares less about who does the killing as long as she harvests the souls. She gets her power from the beast since she is riding the beast.

She is like any earthly leader who gets authority and power from their followers, the military, and other forces that enforce her and the leader's wishes. Babylon's followers give her credence which reinforces her wicked deeds. With no followers, they could do nothing. With no military, they have no power to do their evil deeds. The people today have been brainwashed, consequently they do not think for themselves. They do not consider their actions and go about their military business blindly. They do not seem to consider that without them enforcing these wicked leaders' desires these leaders would not be able to do their evil deeds. **The god of force will be in full play, which is the god the Antichrist will honor.**

In some ways, many of the following Scriptures have been fulfilled. Like many prophetic words, they can be fulfilled more than once. These Scriptures were fulfilled when Nebuchadnezzar sacked Israel and again when Rome took over Israel, burned her, and killed many including Jewish believers.

Why Tribulation

Daniel 11:33, "And **they [mature Overcomers] that understand** among the people shall instruct many: yet they shall **fall by the sword**, and **by flame**, by **captivity**, and by **spoil**, *many* days" (emphasis added).

Daniel 11:35, "And *some* of them of understanding shall fall, **to try them**, [**test**] and **purify them** and to **purge**, and to **make** *them* **white**, *even* to the **time of the end**: because *it is* yet **for a time appointed** [end-times]" (emphasis added).

Those who are going through the testing and remain faithful will be purified, purged, and made white. This verse is especially important for **the time of the end** because it will be the most wicked and hard for those on the earth, especially the believers.

Revelation 2:10, "Fear none of those things which **thou shalt suffer**: behold, **the devil** shall cast *some* of you **into prison**, that ye may be tried; and ye shall have tribulation ten days: be thou **faithful unto death**, and I will give thee a **crown of life**" (emphasis added).

God has all power and authority and He is omnipresent so **He could have easily prevented any and all tribulations.** But **He did not.** Why? Because tribulations are His works. Tribulations put tests and trials into place **for our benefit** so his people can mature and see God at work in their lives. Tests and trials sift those who want to follow the Lord from those who have no desire or are lukewarm towards the Lord. Trials give the Lord's people a chance to see the Lord perform miracles for them. Tests and trials also form the character and personality of the individual. These end-time tests are there to compel us to take our eyes off the world and the lust for the things of this world. Tests and trials show who we are and what's inside of us, what we know and understand.

Hopeful we are meek and that means teachable thereby pliable to the wishes of the Lord as He changes us **into His character.**

The Purpose of Tribulations in Tests and Trials

Daniel 11:35, "And *some* of them **of understanding** shall fall, **to try them**, and **to purge**, and to **make *them*** white, *even* to the **time of the end**: because *it is* yet for a time appointed" (emphasis added).

Daniel 12:10, "Many shall be **purified, and made white**, and tried; but the wicked shall do wickedly: and none of the wicked shall understand; but the wise shall understand" (emphasis added).

Revelation 7:14, "And I said unto him, Sir, thou knowest. And he said to me, These are they which **came out** [they went through the Tribulation] **of great tribulation**, [tests and trials] and have **washed their robes, and made them white** [repentant, faithful, testimony and have been made white] in the blood of the Lamb" (emphasis added).

Revelation 19:14, "And the armies *which were* in heaven followed him [Jesus] upon **white horses**, clothed in fine **linen, white and clean**" (emphasis added).

Early Church Persecution With no Thought of Being Taken Out

Matthew 24:9, "Then shall they deliver you up to be **afflicted and shall kill you**: and ye shall be **hated of all nations** for my name's sake" (emphasis added).

We see persecution in the early church. They suffered and trusted the Lord even unto death. They were purified by tests and trials.

Matthew 10:22, "And ye shall be hated of all *men* for my name's sake: but he that endureth **to the end** shall be saved" (emphasis added).

Mark 13:13, "And ye shall be hated of all *men* for my name's sake: but he that shall endure **unto the end**, the same shall be saved" (emphasis added).

The nations hated them because they followed the Lord. It has always been that way and will be the same during the tribulation. As they hated the Lord, they will hate those who follow Him.

Hebrews 11:35, "Women received their dead raised to life again: and others **were tortured**, not accepting deliverance; that they **might obtain** a **better resurrection**" (emphasis added).

Revelation 18:24, "And in her [Babylon, religion] was found the blood of prophets, and **of saints**, and of **all that were slain upon the earth**" (emphasis added).

All that were slain were slain because of her.

Babylon is the vehicle used to test and purify God's people. The people will be sifted to see who will be faithful and who will not. The tribulation will show if you trust God or not. How much will you suffer and still remain faithful to the Lord? Tribulations are a tool God who is all-powerful, will allow on the earth to see who is really His. **This was all in the plan of God**. Tribulation will compel everyone to come to the Lord or reject the Lord.

In Revelation 17:6, we read, "And I saw the **woman drunken with the blood of the saints**, and with the blood of the **martyrs** of Jesus, and when I saw her, **I wondered** with great admiration" (emphasis added).

Why did John of Revelation wonder with great admiration? John wondered, because she is a mystery, and he **never expected** this woman, this **spirit of religion**, to come upon the earth and **deceive** those who desired to find God. **She was supposed to represent God. She is religion**, and everyone believed that religion, whatever religion, was to help mankind reach and find God, but she is not doing that. She is doing the **exact opposite** as she deceives God's creation with her lies as she steals their soul. Even in Christian groups, many people think their denomination is of God, but are they since they deny the power of God? According to Revelation 17:6, Babylon will come against the true people of God and kill many.

The religious leaders and the god of force, the Roman military, came against Jesus and killed Him. They killed many apostles and many saints. They were not removed from receiving persecution. No, many died. Do you think they will not kill those who want to mature in the things of God in the last days? They killed at the beginning of time as Cain killed righteous Abel, and they will kill again at the end.

The Wrath of Man and the Wrath of God

The wrath of man is influenced by Satan. **During man's wrath, God's people will suffer and mature as they see God working through them and for them**. They will give up all this world has to offer for the sake of others and for Jesus. They will yield in the natural as they learn to trust God in all situations. In the last days, the wrath of man will be the worst ever, because the devil has come down unto the earth having great wrath.

Revelation 12:12, "Therefore rejoice, *ye* heavens, and ye that dwell in them. Woe to the inhabiters of the earth and of the sea! for the **devil is come down unto you**, having great wrath, because he knoweth that he hath but a short time" (emphasis added.

Satan is coming down to the earth to the chaos he has created via wicked men. He is no longer in heaven as our accuser. He has come to possess the Antichrist. This is the wrath that will come upon all of mankind. All men will be tested by the Antichrist to see who they will be faithful to. This will be the hardest time ever for mankind. **This is the wrath of men**. This wrath is brought about by the spirit of Babylon, the Antichrist, and wicked men.

The evil woman, who is the spirit of Babylon, will cause many of God's people to die. So much so that she is drunk with their blood.

Revelation 17:6, "And I saw the woman **drunken with the blood of the saints**, and with the blood of the martyrs of Jesus: and when I saw her, I wondered with great admiration" (emphasis added).

When the Lord returns, the **wrath of God** will come against these evil men, Satan, the Antichrist, and the False Prophet. This wrath of man is different than the wrath of God that God's people are not appointed to. This is explained in my previous book *Unlocking Jesus' Return*.

Luke 21:16, "And ye shall be betrayed both by parents, and brethren, and kinsfolks, and friends; and *some* of you [you, today] shall they cause **to be put to death**" (emphasis added).

John 15:20, "Remember the word that I said unto you, The servant is not greater than his lord. If they have persecuted me, they will **also persecute you**; if they have kept my saying, they will keep yours also" (emphasis added).

Second Timothy 3:12, "Yea, and **all that will live godly** in Christ Jesus **shall suffer persecution**" (emphasis added).

The devil, our adversary, possesses Babylon. He comes to deceive and destroy all of God's people, if possible, and steal their souls if those days were not shortened. Let us read **Jesus' sayings** in Revelation 2:10: "Fear none of those things which **thou shall suffer**: behold **the devil shall cast some of you into prison, that ye may be tried**; and ye shall have tribulation **ten days**: [an appointed amount of time] be thou **faithful 'unto death,'** and I will give thee the **crown of life**" (emphasis added).

Let us remember this is Jesus speaking in the book of Revelation and not some preacher. **The woman, Babylon, will try, test, or purify God's people** as silver and gold are purified during the fire of the tribulation. She will cause many to suffer. Through their suffering, they will call on Jesus. Ten is the complete amount of time allotted for this to continue. It is the total allotted time for her to manifest her wickedness.

It is very clear that God has a purpose for Satan, and that is **to test His people,** and during the testing, they become pure as gold and silver, even if Satan puts them to death. When you see the purpose of Satan, it will not bother you to see yourself going through the tests and trials, even into the tribulation, because a crown of life awaits you.

Will God Take Some People Out Before Others

Will God therefore take some of His people out of this world at the end before they get a chance to be purified and get a crown?

Malachi 3:3, "And he [God] shall sit as a refiner and purifier of silver: and he shall purify the sons of Levi, [Priests of God] and **purge them** as gold and silver, **that they may offer** unto the LORD an offering [offering of ourselves] in righteousness" (emphasis added).

This is the great sacrifice that Moses told Pharaoh he was going to offer to God. The sacrifice is the **offering of self** by God's people. That great sacrifice will be offered on the third day, the third move of God as Moses had stated.

Exodus 5:3, "And they said, The God of the Hebrews hath met with us: let us go, we pray thee, **three days' journey** into the desert, and sacrifice unto the LORD our God; lest he fall upon us with pestilence, or with the sword" (emphasis added).

During this time of purification, the things of this world will become as nothing, worthless, since the world of man controlling man is falling apart. When the kingdoms of men are falling and becoming nothing is the reason why we are to keep our eyes on the Lord and not on the things of this world. Jesus told His disciples that even the temple of God was going to be destroyed. They needed to move from the physical to the higher plain of the spiritual.

Revelation 7:14, "And I said unto him, Sir, thou knowest. And he said to me, These are they which **came out of great tribulation**, and have washed their robes, and made them white in the blood of the Lamb" (emphasis added).

The **International Standard Version says** Revelation 7:14, "I told him, "Sir, you know." Then he told me, "These are the people who are **coming out** of the **terrible suffering**. They have washed their robes and made them white in the blood of the lamb" (emphasis added).

They must have been **in** the tribulation to be able to **come out** of it. How did they come out? They are in heaven wearing white robes, which would lead us to believe they were killed for their testimony.

Revelation 20:4, "And I saw thrones, and they sat upon them, and judgment was given unto them: and *I saw* the souls of them that were **beheaded for the witness of Jesus**, and for the word of God, and which had **not worshipped** the beast, neither his image, neither had received *his* mark upon their foreheads, or in their hands; and **they lived and reigned** with Jesus Christ a thousand years" (emphasis added).

The thousand-year reign is after the tribulation. These saints were killed for the testimony of Jesus during the tribulation. They neither had received *his* mark upon their foreheads or on their hands and were killed.

Many who are on the Earth die today in the Middle East, in Africa, and in other locations for their testimony of Jesus. It can't be any worse for them, even right now since they are dying now as they stay faithful to God with all they have. They offer all they are and have.

The Babylonian beast in religion gets Satan's power to do its wickedness. The beast will have a wicked destructive reign over all the earth. God will use the beast for His purpose. **The beast will destroy all that is exalted of man**, of man's kingdoms, man's religions, and over **every mountain** that man has made. This is the end of man ruling man. This is the end of the Gentiles, the unsaved, and man-ruling man, and of their lifestyles. This is God at work to purify and separate a people.

This is when **every person** will be hot or cold for the Lord. This is the fullness of the Gentiles or the end of the unsaved man, Gentiles. Everyone will have decided to follow the Lord or to follow the beast. All God's people will be saved. The Lord will lose none of His. All others will follow the Antichrist.

God put it in Babylon's heart to destroy mankind's mountains, religions, businesses, and governments because they did not seek God or give Him His rightful place, nor did they give Him the glory He deserved. After the Antichrist has used Babylon and has no more use for it, he will have her destroyed and burned. This will be his attempt at destroying all religions on the earth. He will want to be worshipped as God and no other religion's God will be tolerated.

Towards the end of the thousand-year reign of Jesus, God sent His angel to release this demon from the bottomless pit. In other words, **God is using** this **demonic entity, the Destroyer**, to do His work, and that is **to destroy** man's position of exalting himself to the place of God instead of God being the ruler and Lord. This is again as the Tower of Babylon where mankind was exalting himself to the place of God. God will have had enough of this and He will now set up His kingdom.

Tribulation

Tribulation is a time of sifting. No man in the natural can survive it. But he can if he **lives in the supernatural** with God. You will have to be hot for God or you will be cold. You will have to live by the supernatural, above the natural realm, as Israel did for forty years in the desert and as Elijah and Jesus did. You must **now** learn to **live in the supernatural**.

Jesus said in John 14:12, "Verily, verily, I say unto you, He that believeth on me, the works that I do shall he do also; and greater *works* than these shall he do; because I go unto my Father. This Scripture must be fulfilled. Jesus multiplied the fish and the loaves supernaturally, and thousands were fed and drew near to hear Him. So shall it be again as the Overcomers supernaturally minister to God's people.

Elijah must return **before** the great and **dreadful day** of the Lord. The Overcomers will have the spirit that was on Elijah. They are the fulfillment of the return of Elijah. They will be on the earth when God allows the destruction of all the man-made kingdoms.

Revelation 17:17, For **God hath put in their hearts** to fulfil **his will**, and to agree, and give their kingdom [the people's businesses or mountain] unto the beast, **until the words of God shall be fulfilled**" (emphasis added).

Tribulation is God's idea, as it was to crucify Jesus Christ. He is not interested in maintaining the kingdoms of men. He is interested in our spiritual maturity and His kingdom.

All these tribulations we have in our lives is to change our character, our thinking, and our way of life so we may become what God has for us. We are to become mature to the fullness of Christ. He will have His vision and destiny fulfilled. We must come to the place where we trust the Lord for and in all things. We must realize the Lord is truly the Lord, and we are His creation, His sons and daughters, and are to be obedient to him.

The Lord said pray in Matthew 6:10, "Thy kingdom come. Thy will be done in earth, as *it is* in heaven" (emphasis added).

He did not say to do your will but to do God's will on the earth as it is in heaven.

Revelation 17:12 repeats and continues with the explanation, "And the ten horns are ten kings which have received **no kingdom as yet**, but receive **power as kings one hour** with the beast" [Antichrist] (emphasis added).

Ten means the total **complete number** of this group, **whatever the quantity** is **in this natural realm**. Ten pertains to this natural realm.

Horns symbolize power. They will have the total amount of power in the natural realm that is to be given to them, whatever that is. These are wicked leaders who are as kings but are not in existence yet since they have no kingdom until the beast manifests; then they will individually receive a kingdom and power.

Kings are dictators who rule with supreme power over people and land. These dictators have no specific country, but they will eventually have power over specific areas. The dictators will receive power when the eighth, the beast, comes into power. This will be for a short time since it is for only **one hour**. These horns are against God and His people and thus are **antichrist in spirit**.

These dictators really have no kingdom, no country, or no territory of their own. They will be given a kingdom of some kind; perhaps it could be a new division of the earth. Or will it be over a certain group of people or perhaps one of the trading blocks of the world that some exalted men have divided for these dictators to control? The Club of Rome, a powerful secret club, has already divided the world into ten administrative regions.

Daniel 11:39, "Thus shall he [Antichrist] do in the most strongholds with a strange god, whom he shall acknowledge *and* increase with glory: and he shall cause them to **rule over many**, and shall **divide the land** for gain" (emphasis added).

The beast and the dictators will have power for a short time, symbolized by the words "one hour." The kings are used by Satan to steal the earth and the souls from mankind. The kings do not comprehend the deception of this evil spirit. Those written in the Book of Life from the foundation of the world have knowledge of what is going on and will escape their deceptions. They will need to continually seek the Lord.

Those not written in the book from the foundation of the world are therefore not from the descendants of Adam and **not legally** on the earth. Are they from the seed of the Serpent, Satan as Genesis tells? Are they the tares Jesus spoke of?

The beast is used to test God's people, even unto death. They will be tested to see if they are hot or cold. Do they love the world and the things of the world more than Jesus? Will they give their very life for the Lord?

This group of ten leaders will be very strong and determined as Revelation 17:13 says, "These have **one mind**, and shall give their power and strength unto the beast" (emphasis added).

The beast will need great physical power to fulfill his desires. He will organize with these other evil spiritual leaders. They will represent **a many-member body or group.** They are of one mind with the beast. They will give the beast their power by deceiving and forcing their followers to believe in them and in the beast. They will enforce their desires and the beast's desires on their followers. To have followers is what gives them power. Without followers, these leaders have no power.

Without the followers, the beast will have no great power. These horns of power, these dictators, will be of one mind with the beast. They will have the same goal, and the same desires as the beast. They will back up the beast to fulfill his desires. The beast wants to control everyone and wants to be exalted to the place of God. These leaders will do all they can to see the beast's vision come to pass. **This beast wants to be exalted as God as a fulfillment of the Tower of Babylon.**

The ultimate desire of the beast is to take the place of God **and steal men's souls and the earth**. He wants **to eliminate** any and all who represent **any other kind of religion or gods**. The woman, religion, **thinks** they are in agreement with her since she is riding the horns and the beast, but she is mistaken, as we shall see.

To show that Babylon is in various religions let us read Revelation 17:15, "And he saith unto me, **the waters** which thou sawest **where the whore sitteth, are people**, and **multitudes**, and **nations**, and **tongues**" (emphasis added).

The waters symbolize the people upon which Babylon, the whore, religion, is sitting upon. She is controlling, carried by, or subjecting the people to their man-made religions, her thinking. Man-made religions are the only thing that is **all over the earth. The people of the world are the ones who promoted and "give life" and power to their various religions**. They carry or cause religions to have their existence. Without these religions and their rituals, the people inside them would be free to find God. This is true of all religions in every part of the world. Without people, that religion would cease. **The people are the power behind these man-made religions, thus Babylon.**

There is but one true religion and that is the one which God gave. God started with Abraham who believed and obeyed God. He walked by faith and obeyed God. He trusted God. He had a true relationship with God. Moses then came and expounded the ways that God desired. King David had a personal relationship with God even though he sinned. Jesus emphasized and completed God's religion. He walked in love as He gave Himself for the sins of men as He obeyed the Father. He walked in the Spirit. He is the Way, and we are to follow. We must have soft hearts, be obedient, and walk in the Spirit as God leads. The law of the Old Testament was to show us we can't do it with the ability of the flesh. We must submit and humble ourselves to God's Spirit. Get a soft teachable heart and receive from God. Be led by the Spirit of God.

The Scripture tells us the woman is sitting on the head of these horns, these leaders as we saw in verse 9, imply that the woman has a domineering position over them, **lording over them.** From that position, the people **can be threatened** with going to heaven or hell, put in bondage or killed, which is done today. The horns will eventually hate her control over them and will **destroy her** as we see in verse 16: "And the **ten horns** which thou sawest upon the beast, these shall **hate** the whore, and shall make **her desolate and naked**, and shall eat her flesh, and burn her with fire" (emphasis added). The people are following the whore, religions, Babylon, and are not following the horns which are the kings who do not like that. They will destroy the whore and when she is destroyed the people are persecuted and scattered out of their religions.

The beast, the whore, and the ten horns are not the same. The ten horns, which are the ten dictators, will eventually hate the whore, Babylon, the religions of the world. Remember that Babylon is sitting on top of them. The kings, the dictators, hate the whore, which is religion, because she is controlling and lording over them. She puts pressure on them for them to do her desires. The horns will eventually destroy the woman because she represents religion and since the **beast wants to be God** and does not want any other religion, he will have her destroyed. In other words, persecution will happen in **all religions of the world**.

The ten horns will pursue the whore in order to destroy her. **All man-made religions** will be persecuted and destroyed. The horns will ultimately persecute all religions, including God's true mature people since the beast will want to be exalted as God. These worldly leaders will turn against Babylon, religion, hate her, and destroy her with fire. She will be stripped, her people killed or dispersed, and they will burn her. To burn her is to emphasize that she will no longer rise. All religions will be destroyed and burned. They will disappear.

This is perhaps also the burning of physical structures and the like as well as chasing the people out of them, eating her flesh, making her desolate without people.

Revelation 17:17–18, "For **God hath put** in their hearts to fulfil His will, and to agree, and give their kingdom unto the beast, until the words of God shall be fulfilled.

And **the woman** which thou sawest is that great city which **reigneth over the kings of the earth**" (emphasis added).

The great city is not a physical city but the totality of what Babylon controls over the whole earth. How does she reign over kings? By putting fear in them as though she has the power of heaven and hell and as to where one goes after they die. In the beginning she will have the power to threaten these leaders also.

God put it in the heart of the beast and the horns to do His will, which is to destroy all man-made religions that have continually hindered God's people from maturing and from ministering. Religious followers are given man-made commandments that hinder God's true people from keeping God's commandments, teachings, the feasts, and from maturing in the things of God.

The beast will want to destroy all religions because he will want to be exalted as God. He, being the eighth as we have seen, is now the main religious leader on earth other than God. No longer will any other religion be tolerated, which is why they are destroyed. He wants to be in everyone's heart and on the throne of everyone's life as a dictator. The setting up of the spirit of the Antichrist in the heart of everyone will be the **abomination that maketh desolate**. To be **desolate is to be lost without hope**. This is the fulfillment, the result of taking the mark of the beast which is to follow the Antichrist with all your heart. This is being against Jesus Christ.

Daniel 11:31, "And arms shall stand on his part, and they shall **pollute the sanctuary** of strength, and shall take away the **daily** *sacrifice*, and they shall place the abomination that **maketh desolate**" (emphasis added).

If another temple is built in Israel, this third beast will exalt himself as God in the temple. He will eventually stop all offerings of sacrifices the priests offer to God. God will not honor these sacrifices of animals since Jesus Christ was the perfect sacrifice. The Antichrist will also desecrate the physical temple.

The believers' strength is in the Lord. He resides in us. We are His sanctuary. If you pollute your sanctuary with pornography, hatred, unforgiveness, murder, and such sins, you will then lose favor with God. The daily sacrifice offered to God is for God's people to follow the Lord daily. We are to die daily. To "take it away" is to be forced to do something else other than what God wants. Some **former believers** will give place to these abominations in their lives, thinking that grace will cover these willful sins. Consequently, this will make their lives desolate and pollute their souls, their sanctuaries where God is to dwell. This will allow an open door for sin to come in and for them to fall and perhaps even lose their souls.

Daniel 11:36, "And the king shall **do according to his will**; and he shall exalt himself, and magnify himself **above every god**, and shall speak marvellous things **against the God** of gods and shall prosper [successful] till [until] the indignation be accomplished: for that that is determined shall be done" (emphasis added).

119

At the **very end,** the beast and his followers will come against Jesus and His followers as we see in Revelation 17:14, "These shall **make war with the Lamb**, and the Lamb shall overcome them: for He is Lord of lords, and King of kings: and they that are with him are **called, and chosen, and faithful**" (emphasis added).

The Lamb and those with Him will defeat the beast and its ten heads. The Lamb, as we all know, is symbolic of Jesus Christ.

God Will Have a People

There will be people who are fully matured Christians and who are **on the earth at this time.** They will have totally died to self, to their personal desires, to the world, and are filled with the Holy Ghost. Jesus will be working 100 percent through them. Jesus was the fullness of the Father, even though He had a body of flesh on the earth. These mature Christians will be the fullness of Jesus Christ and they will fulfill the many Scriptures that have yet to be fulfilled. They will be called Overcomers, the Remnant. The Holy Ghost will be their guide and He will be their comforter. They will know His voice and obey it.

"As **He is,** so are we **in this world**" (1 John 4:17, emphasis added).

When Saul was persecuting the church, the Lord said to him in "Act 9:4, "And he fell to the earth, and heard a voice saying unto him, Saul, Saul, why persecutest thou me?" Saul was persecuting God's people, but the Lord considered it to be the same as persecuting Him personally. We are His body.

These mature people will be one with the Lord. The Lord Jesus will personally, or the Lord Jesus through His mature Christians, will overcome the beast and his dictators. Those with the Lamb are: 1) called, 2) chosen, and 3) faithful, just like Jesus is. **Today many are called, but few are chosen,** but how many will **stay faithful**? Are you one with Jesus now? These are also referred to as the remnant.

The mature people of God will be one with the Lord of lords and the King of kings. Will they stay faithful to God if they see their children hurt or someone they love killed? We have to trust God in all situations, no matter what the results look like, **even unto death. He has our best spiritual interest at hand.**

Revelation 2:26–27, "And he that **overcometh**, and keepeth my works **unto the end**, to him [*overcomer*] will I give power **over the nations**

"And he [overcomer] shall rule them with a rod of iron; as the vessels of a potter shall they be broken to shivers: **even as I received of my Father**" (emphasis added).

God's people, the Overcomers, are doing mighty exploits as they do the works of Jesus Christ. They will rule the nations as directed by the Spirit of God.

The true people of God will manifest the works of Jesus and will instruct many. Some will be persecuted and killed, and some will willingly lay their lives down while others will be protected. Some will be protected during this time as was Noah protected during the flood, and as God's people were protected in Egypt during the plagues that came upon the Egyptians. In all cases, our lives are in God's hands to do **as He desires**. We must **trust** Him and believe that whatever happens is best for our spiritual maturity.

The Scripture "Thy kingdom come thy will be done on earth as it is in heaven" will become a reality.

Who Is Jesus?

God the Father took of Himself, who He is, His love, His character and all His attributes and put it in a baby called Jesus. He was truly the Father of Jesus. Jesus was from the Father. When Jesus said that God was His Father He was not lying. He was the Father of Jesus in every way. The baby was a man. He had all the weaknesses of man, making Jesus as a man. He was all God and yet man. The mystery of mysteries.

Jesus was not from Joseph. No! He was totally conceived of God the Father by the Holy Spirit. That which made up Jesus was all part of God the Father. That is why Jesus is God because He was all made of what God is. That is why Jesus could say that He was One with the Father because He really was. He was the Son of God, the only begotten (gotten) Son. He was the **only** Son that God has had. He was totally made up of what God is. That is why He could say, "If you have seen Me, you have seen the Father."

Jesus had access to the spiritual realm from which He continually saw the Father and what He did.

When Jesus died on the cross, He was not just a man dying on the cross. He was extremely special because it was the only Son of God dying on the cross for you and me. That is why this great sacrifice was the **only** acceptable sacrifice that could pay for your sins and mine.

When a person accepts the gift of Jesus paying for their sins it really is something supernatural. When you accept Jesus and His love, you become a new creation.

Now, Jesus desires us to follow Him not only in deeds or our lifestyle but also spiritually. We need to grow up spiritually to be able to attain that position. He desires for us to enter into that spiritual realm. His Word says some will enter into this spiritual maturity and fulfill His desire for us to be one with Him and with the Father as He was one with the Father.

Will we be one of them?

End Times Scenario

Six is the number of man or Satan's influence on man. Six plus Six is man controlling man who is influenced by evil spirits as man makes all the decisions for himself without God.

Mankind is getting more and more evil every day. Still, God is patient and keeps His hand of protection and blessings over mankind as He blesses them.

God will allow this rebellion to continue for a certain amount of time. At the end of the time allotted for mankind to repent God will remove His hand of protection and the blessings from man if man has not repented. When the hand of blessing is removed, the curses come upon you. The curses are famines, wars, earthquakes, and various disasters.

If this evil continues, He will remove His hand and let wicked men come against one another. Wars will pop up in various places. Political leaders will not be able to solve these many problems even though they will promise to improve the world's situation.

With God's hand of blessings lifted, all this chaos, wars, disasters, famines, pests, and confusion will be manifested to bring man to his end. This will be the culmination of the wickedness of man as a beast. This can be seen in King Nebuchadnezzar who became a beast because he did not acknowledge that God is God.

This will be **the end of man ruling man** as we know it today. That will be the end of the world as we know it as the antichrist, man sits on the throne and rules the world. He will rule for the time he has been allotted until Jesus returns and deposes these evil leaders.

The spirit of Satan will come out of the beast, the eighth king, who is the antichrist when Jesus returns. Then, the antichrist and the false prophet are cast into the Lake of Fire but not Satan. Satan will be cast into the Lake of Fire later.

Revelation 16:13, "And I saw three **unclean spirits** like frogs come out of the mouth of the **dragon**, [Satan] and out of the mouth of the **beast**, [antichrist] and out of the mouth of the false prophet" (emphasis added).

Revelation 19:20, "And the beast [antichrist] was taken and with him the false prophet that wrought miracles before him, with which he deceived them that had received the mark of the beast, [antichrist] and them that worshipped his image. These **both** [but not Satan] were cast alive into a lake of fire burning with brimstone" (emphasis added).

Revelation 20:2–3, "And he laid hold on the dragon, that old serpent, which is the Devil, and Satan, and bound him a thousand years,

"And cast him into the bottomless pit, and shut him up, and set a seal upon him, that he should deceive the nations no more, till the thousand years should be fulfilled: and after that he must be loosed a little season."

Later, after the Thousand Year reign of Jesus is nearly completed Satan is released from the pit to tempt man again to see who are God's people and who are his followers. Satan and his followers will be destroyed by Jesus upon His arrival. Satan will be cast into the Lake of Fire where the beast and the false prophet are enjoying the heat.

Revelation 20:10, "And the devil that deceived them was cast into the lake of fire and brimstone, where the beast and the false prophet are, and shall be tormented day and night for ever and ever.

Only those who truly repent and change from their wicked ways shall be protected but persecuted by those who do not desire to follow and honor our God and Lord.

In the end, the manifestation of true wickedness will be exposed as the antichrist is revealed. False teachings will increase along with false prophets. Lies and deceit will be multiplied so much that you will not be able to trust anyone. Children will betray their parents and the parents their children.

The lust for this world must be removed from your life in order to completely give your life to the Lord Jesus Christ. Jesus said to the rich man in Luke 18:22, "Now when Jesus heard these things, he said unto him, Yet lackest thou one thing: sell all that thou hast, and distribute unto the poor, and thou shalt have treasure in heaven: and come, follow me."

God is the same today, tomorrow, and forever.

Abraham was told to leave his country and go to a place he did not know. This is where he saw a city not made with hands, New Jerusalem. THE LOVE FOR THIS WORLD WILL HAVE TO BE FORGOTTEN SINCE THE KINGDOMS OF MAN ARE FALLING APART, NEVER TO RETURN. THE LOVE OF JESUS MUST INCREASE LIKE NEVER BEFORE. THEN WE WILL OVERCOME.

World Ambassadors for Christ
Justin Douziech

About the Author

Justin Douziech is the founder and president of World Ambassadors for Christ. He went to Omega Bible School in San Jose, California. During and prior to this time he also worked for Nora Lam Ministry for three years. He helped her organize crusades and traveled to the Orient. While at the Bible school he met his beautiful wife, Evelyn, got married, and went to Mexico where they ministered. Later he and his wife co-pastored with Pastor Ralph Wilkerson at Melodyland, a church of ten thousand. There they continued to learn how to walk in the spirit. They have started churches in Mexico, the U.S., the Philippines, and Canada. He is the author *Antichrist and the Third Day Overcomers, Unlocking Jesus Return,* and now this new book, *Unlocking the Mystery of Babylon.*

References

Authorized King James Bible
1975
The Open Bible Edition
Nashville, Tennessee
Thomas Nelson Inc., Publishers
KJV copied from e-sword
Babel (in the Strong Concordance #H895,) appears 246 times in the Old Testament

Webster's Dictionary says that Babylon was a city devoted to **materialism** and the pursuit of **sensual pleasure.**

www.ingramcontent.com/pod-product-compliance
Lightning Source LLC
Chambersburg PA
CBHW061147040426
42445CB00013B/1600